Dining Car Line
to the Pacific

Dining Car Line
to the Pacific

AN ILLUSTRATED HISTORY
OF THE NP RAILWAY'S
"FAMOUSLY GOOD" FOOD,
WITH 150 AUTHENTIC RECIPES

William A. McKenzie

Minnesota Historical Society Press • St. Paul

MINNESOTA HISTORICAL SOCIETY PRESS, St. Paul 55101

∞ The paper used in this publication meets the minimum requirements of the American National Standard for Information Sciences— Permanence for Printed Library Materials, ANSI Z39.48-1984.

Manufactured in the United States of America
10 9 8 7 6 5 4 3 2 1

International Standard Book Number   0-87351-253-7 Cloth
                                            0-87351-254-5 Paper

Library of Congress Cataloging-in-Publication Data

McKenzie, William A., 1926-
    Dining car line to the Pacific : an illustrated history of the NP Railway's "famously good" food, with 150 authentic recipes / William A. McKenzie.
      p. cm.
    Includes bibliographical references (p.).
    ISBN 0-87351-253-7 (alk. paper). ISBN 0-87351-254-5 (pbk.)
    1. Railroads—United States—Dining-car service. 2. Northern Pacific Railway Company. I. Title.
    TF668.M38 1990
    625.2'3—dc20   89-27960
                         CIP

PICTURE CREDITS

Unless otherwise noted below, the photographs reproduced in this book are owned by the author. Taken by NP photographers, they are used with the permission of Burlington Northern Inc.

Photographs and other images on the following pages appear through the courtesy of the persons and institutions listed below. The names of the photographers, when known, are indicated in parentheses.

Pages 4, 74 bottom—collection of John E. Foote
Pages 5, 19, 51, 72, 73, 83, 95, 96—Northern Pacific Railway Records, Minnesota Historical Society
Pages 6 bottom, 14, 18, 105, 107, 108—Don L. Hofsommer photos
Pages 31 (B. F. Upton), 33, 34, 35 (W. H. Illingworth), 37 (drawing by A. R. Waud), 40 (W. H. Illingworth), 41 (Haynes Studios, Inc.), 45, 47, 59 left (William H. Jacoby), right, top & middle (Schlattman Bros.), bottom (W. H. Illingworth),   68 top—Audio-Visual Library, Minnesota Historical Society
Page 39—NP photograph; copy courtesy of Wayne C. Olsen
Pages 43 (F. Jay Haynes), 54 (Elliott W. Hunter), 57 (F. Jay Haynes)—Haynes Foundation Collection, Montana Historical Society
Page 74 top—courtesy of Franklyn F. Perrin

Original illustrations by Mary Sandberg

A cook they had with them for the nonce,
To boil up the chickens with the marrow bones
And flavor tartly as with galingale.
He could discern the taste of London ale.
He could roast, and seethe, and broil, and fry,
Make hearty soup and bake good pie . . .
As for blanc-manger, he made it with the best.

Geoffrey Chaucer, *Canterbury Tales*

Contents

Some Personal Observations

For most of us who regard ourselves as veteran wayfarers, travel and food are as inseparable as Moses and the bulrushes, Antony and Cleopatra, Holmes and Watson, Hope and Crosby, the Lone Ranger and Tonto, Garrison Keillor and Lake Wobegon, or—more to the point—the Northern Pacific and the Great Big Baked Potato. True, each of these, with the rather obvious exception of Keillor's imaginary Minnesota village, could have survived as a viable, independent entity. But they all made the greatest impact when they were linked with each other. Especially—and here I readily admit to great bias— the railroad and the mammoth tuber. I claim, as well, that the world is filled with people willing to join me in trumpeting the surpassing enjoyment of a trip in the company of western scenery; an amiable steward; friendly, efficient, and immaculately clad waiters; and food right out of a dream.

Little survives of this dream for the peripatetic gastronomes who rose to the zenith of gratification in the aromatic ambience of "dinner in the diner." This is true even if one takes a charitable view of Amtrak's basic repasts and those reheated offerings of the airlines. Passengers today who want more than subsistence-level food must eat during stopovers and fantasize about the time when dining cars filled more than one kind of void.

However, little has been written to help travelers get the picture fairly in mind; bibliographies on the subject are undernourished in the extreme. Nowhere—not in hobby shops, libraries or private collections, or advertised in railfan publications—could I find a single volume devoted to the history of American dining car service from its legitimate birth in 1868 up to 1971, when Amtrak (under the National Railroad Passenger Corporation) took over a moribund service from a railroad industry wearied by growing deficits. Those interested in ceramics can easily find a minutely researched work on dining car china written by a noted collector expressly for other collectors, whose name is legion. And there are several good histories of the origin and evolution of rolling stock, such as the monumental opus of John W. White, Jr., *The American Railroad Passenger Car*. Will C. Hollister's brief but useful account, *Dinner in the Diner*, surveys the outstanding recipes among famous trains of selected railroads. It provides skeletal histories and publishes recipes (untested by the author) that were provided by railroads in response to form-letter inquiries. Countless other writers and authors have given us glowing accounts, by and large, of their experiences in dream dining cars on various classic trains; but as a rule, these run to no more than a few thousand words.[1]

Until now, the story behind the scenes has not been told. The development of the dining car service; food procurement and preparation; the people who directed the operation and those who prepared and served the food; the ways the service was used to promote the railroad—these topics usually appear only in passing references to their impact on gross passenger income and, ultimately, on the balance sheet.

Dining Car Line to the Pacific does not begin to exhaust the subject. It offers no itemized history of Northern Pacific china; it does not include plans and photos of all the dining cars acquired by the company, or rosters of their personnel. Instead, it is a verbal and selective pictorial pageant written for those who would rekindle the old flame of endearing and memorable times aboard NP dining cars, and no more.

Even so, I commend it to those who would find pleasure in the recounting of an almost legendary period in the lives of American travelers, an era that fueled keen emotions and appealed to the latent hedonism in most of us. We enjoy being coddled. On NP dining cars, to serve properly was to coddle much. In this veteran's view, no other railroad, try as it might, could boast of having coddled so well. What NP chefs and their cooks were able to achieve in the cramped confines of their kitchens, each and every mealtime on their trains, was little less than a miracle. For untold millions they produced a crowning touch to every trip via the pioneer northern route.

Many who are familiar with the history of our transcontinental railroads as it appears in school textbooks will be surprised to learn that the Northern Pacific could justly claim that it was *the* "Dining Car Line to the Pacific." Between 1883, when the company completed its line to the West Coast, and 1889, when the 20-year-old Union Pacific concluded it was losing too much business to this northern upstart, the NP was the only transcontinental that operated dining cars in regular daily passenger service.

The man responsible for this surprise was Henry Villard, a railroad builder of high integrity whose success, I contend, continues to be ignored, and whose reputation, as a result, suffers grievously at the hands of historians more gifted in fiction and sensationalism than in sticking to the unvarnished truth. His successors left its nurturing and development in the hands of "the operating and passenger people," to whom we owe some gratitude. Although they failed to grasp the value of dining car service as a competitive tool in its own right, they had the good sense to maintain its quality at a consistently high level. Then, near the end of the first decade of the 20th century, Hazen J. Titus made the Northern Pacific dining experience different from all the others. The careers of all these men are part of the larger story that follows.

Every effort has been made to ensure that the recipes contained herein have retained all of their original characteristics, with nothing added or taken away, except where necessary. They were originally written for chefs who had to prepare dishes in large quantities. It is not enough merely to divide the ingredients for a dish for 48 by eight to determine the proper amounts when you want to serve only six. Some ingredients must be present in greater strength to stand out in a crowd. As the crowd thins, they will be at their best when reduced proportionately lower. The only way to be certain of that level is to test and retest a recipe until it produces results that measure up to the original.

Although I have been counted as one who often has a way with food, I usually make a production out of every cooking project. On the other hand, my wife, Violet, has a knack for achieving equally good and often better results without ruffles and flourishes. She tends to reach her goals intuitively and, therefore, more quickly than I. So in her capable hands was placed the enormous job of testing each recipe—and retesting it, if necessary—to make sure it was right, as well as of writing it in language all of us can understand today.

NP chefs in times long gone were schooled to read recipes that called for a kitchen spoon (about four tablespoons) of *this* and a gill (four liquid ounces) of *that*, then to strain everything through a China cap (a conical strainer six or more inches in diameter and six to eight inches deep, now referred to as a Chinese strainer) before serving in a *Bain-Marie* (a three-piece chef's utensil made of china, the bottom part filled with hot water for keeping sauces warm—like a double boiler).[2] All such words and terms have been translated into today's household idiom, and all measurements have been made as precise as practicable. Although a bit of flavor may have been lost in translation, we have made every effort to see that the food survives in the original.

Acknowledgments

Any work of authentic history is, essentially, a collaboration for which the author unjustly receives most of the credit. To remedy that miscarriage of justice, in this instance, at least, I must express my gratitude to many "co-laborers," but especially to my wife, Violet, without whose help the book could not have been written. She is, in fact, its co-author, having selected, tested, and written all the recipes that are an integral part of it. But beyond this, she provided inspiration and unfailing support, as well as critical comment of great value. The list of those who contributed material help is quite long. William F. Paar (now deceased), Robert Jones, Richard E. Carlson, Leon Hampton, Dexter Pugh, and Littleton Gardner, all former members of Northern Pacific Railway's dining car department, whose careers spanned the period from 1912 to 1970, kindly consented to be interviewed, some more than once. And Mr. Paar provided recipes and instruction bulletins that were indispensable to the work.

Ruby Shields, Ruth Bauer, and Steve Nielsen, reference archivists at the Minnesota Historical Society's Division of Library and Archives, helped me find my way through the labyrinth of files in the NP collection, of which the society is now the custodian.

My debt to Don L. Hofsommer is incalculable. First and foremost my most persistent gadfly, he was the prime "outside" reader of the manuscript. From that reading he produced several pages of necessary corrections and sound advice. Not content with all that, he offered the use of everything in a collection of photos he made, both at the Northern Pacific commissary and on board dining cars.

John E. Foote opened for me the doors of his home and the gates to his dazzling collection of NP artifacts and memorabilia, much of it dealing with the dining car service. Richard C. Bressler and Allan Boyce, of Burlington Northern Inc., graciously granted permission to use photographs from the BN collection, many of which came from former NP files. For their unstinting support and encouragement I am in eternal debt to Franklyn F. Perrin, Walter A. Gustafson, Louis W. Menk, Norman M. Lorentzsen, Walter Baillon, John Willard, Patrick W. Stafford, and Kim Forman.

A particularly special blessing for me, and one I would wish for all first-book authors, is a caring publisher. Minnesota Historical Society Press is that, and more. John McGuigan, former managing editor, and Ann Regan, his worthy successor, not only made me feel like one of the family, but also they provided the kind of editorial and personal support that I once believed was reserved for a rather small stable of best-selling authors whose work is handled easily and profitably. My thanks, as great as they are, seem inadequate.

Now, after having apparently divulged all my accounts payable, I must confess I have another that may total more than all the others. It is not an exaggeration to say that I would never even have begun work on this book but for the faith and confidence in me that was shown and expressed by one man nearly 35 years ago. He became my mentor, my editor, my idol, and my friend. I would have him as a father. This is the late L. L. Perrin, to whom this book is respectfully, nay, lovingly, dedicated.

A Trip in a Dining Car

I

T WAS MID-MORNING IN MID-JULY in the mid-1960s. Fluffy cumulus clouds drifted to the southeast in leisurely fashion, seemingly reluctant to take leave of the Mississippi River that flowed placidly between high white bluffs below. The air was unseasonably cool for a Minnesota summer, and quite still, smelling faintly of diesel locomotive exhaust with a hint of freshly baked bread. A flock of pigeons thrummed into the sky, startled by an automobile that came crackling over a cindered road leading from a little-used pavement toward a long, nondescript, two-story brick building that flanked several parallel lines of railroad tracks filled with passenger cars. High above the building's flat roof towered a skeletal steel framework to which were affixed individual neon letters that spelled out the message, "4-Dome Train West" and "North Coast Limited." At the top and slightly off-center was a six-foot-diameter reproduction of the ancient Oriental monad, trademark of the Northern Pacific Railway.

The railroad tracks, totaling six miles of storage, repair, and servicing areas, comprised the Northern Pacific's Third Street Coach Yards in St. Paul; the building was the Northern Pacific's commissary; and the driver of the automobile was Robert J. (Bob) Jones, one of the Northern Pacific's dining car stewards. Yards and building had been in service since 1926, just over 40 years, and Bob Jones had been in the dining car service for about 24 years.[1] He had been a steward since 1963. What set him apart from the majority of his fellow stewards was the fact that he was black, and what set the NP's dining car service apart from every other western railroad's was the fact that it was the first to operate all the way from the middle of the continent to the West Coast.

Jones parked his car just north of the building beside those of other commissary employees in an area that was almost devoid of cinders, those remnants of the days when coal-burning, steam locomotives powered the company's freight and passenger trains. He was reporting in a few minutes before his crew of four cooks and six waiters was scheduled to stock their car for a next-day departure to Chicago. What follows is a true-to-life account of what might have gone into one of his typical trips on a Northern Pacific dining car.

"I always had business with Bill Paar [superintendent of the dining car department] or the assistant superintendent regarding the trip," he remembers. "We'd get our letters on who we would encounter—what group or groups—in the course of the trip. And, then," he adds, "whether there'd been any problem out there on the previous trip." [2]

One such "problem" letter, which Jones had received some months earlier, had been curt to the point of insult. Or so it may have seemed to one unacquainted with its writer: "Order enough supplies out of the commissary. You're receiving too many supplies along the line." That was all. And it was signed, simply, "W. F. Paar." There had been no salutation, no complimentary close.[3] Although it rankled a bit, to Jones it was part of a familiar routine in which the head man sought, quite needlessly, to keep him on his toes for the good of the service. In this respect, Paar and Jones were of one mind.

This morning, a letter from Paar might inform Bob Jones that the directors of the Rainier National Park Company and their wives, a group of 14, would ride the Vista-Dome *North Coast Limited* from Tacoma, Washington, to Livingston, Montana, for a tour of Yellowstone National Park. On the same train, there would be a group of 44 high-school students and their chaperones traveling from Portland to Chicago on their way east to visit historic sites at Washington, D.C.; Williamsburg, Yorktown, and Jamestown, Virginia; Philadelphia; New York City; Boston, Lexington, and Concord, Massachusetts; and Detroit, Michigan. In addition, there could be a copy of a short letter to Paar from Walter A. Gustafson, manager of advertising and publicity, announcing that the travel editor of the *Chicago Tribune*, William W. Yates, would board the train at Chicago the following day for a trip to Seattle on the first leg of a circle tour that would acquaint him with most of the "name trains" among western railroads. He was to be served his choice of dinner the first day out, compliments of Mr. Gustafson.

This often confusing mix of superfluous with necessary detail was characteristic of Paar's letters to his stewards. But to Paar, all the information was essential if his crews were to provide the kind of personal service he demanded. In any case, it gave Jones time to prepare for the return trip: there would be no ordering of extra supplies in St. Paul; that would come at Seattle three days later. For now, he had only to check with the passenger department to learn how many reservations had been made for the westbound trip and to order his supplies accordingly.

All passenger space on the *North Coast Limited*, whether coach seat or Pullman accommodation, was assigned by reservation only. Therefore, a fairly accurate head count was available at stocking time. The steward had only to add a dozen or so to the figures furnished by the general passenger agent to be prepared for those who might make reservations on the day of departure. Once in a while, of course, this rule of thumb did not apply, and a steward would be faced with more dining guests than he had anticipated. For example, there might be some special event for which a low estimate had been made, like the one that had elicited Paar's reproving letter. In that case, the annual Western Days celebration in Billings attracted a

The St. Paul railyards, 1931, with NP commissary and coach yard in foreground

Menus were sometimes printed for special parties.

larger number of additional passengers out of Glendive, Miles City, and Forsyth, Montana, than had been predicted. As a result, the 37 additional seatings for the next morning's breakfast meant the dining car would be woefully short of eggs, bacon, ham, sausage, breakfast steak, milk, coffee, juice, toasting bread, and sweet rolls as the train approached Seattle. To make up the shortage Jones had detrained at Billings to order replenishments from the lunchroom at Missoula, Montana. And therein lies another tale: the reason why the NP continued to operate on-line restaurants long after the apparent need for them had vanished with the introduction of dining car service in 1883.

Most NP restaurants had been established at main-line stations that also were junction points for branch-line rail service. This meant that branch-line passengers who were destined to some other station on the main line could buy meals while they awaited the arrival of their trains. These stations were also, in almost all cases, crew-change points. Therefore, NP train crews who were turning around could "hit the beanery" while they waited. Although lodging for train crews was provided at company expense where needed, meals were out-of-pocket expenditures for the employees. Lunchrooms made it possible for them to buy balanced meals, if they wished, at prices that were competitive with, or even less expensive than, those charged for "beans" at locally owned restaurants. Then, of course, there was the profit motive.

Unlike the dining cars, NP lunchrooms rarely were operated at a loss. The latter were nowhere near as labor-intensive; a manager, one or two cooks, and two or three waiters or waitresses, all of whom were local residents who occasioned no expenditure for overnight lodgings in distant cities, made fewer inroads on gross income. Neither did the department attempt to offer haute cuisine in the lunchrooms—except in that earlier day, where the company had built and operated a number of fine hotels.

Good, hearty meals, well prepared and economical, were the rule in lunchrooms, for which separate menus were printed and different recipes were supplied. Consequently, more gross income was brought down to profit. This helped to offset, to a limited extent, the daily losses of the cars.

Finally, there was the convenience of having what might be called backup commissaries at many points where stewards could replenish their supplies when the dining cars were running low. If you were the superintendent, however, and you wished top management to know that you were making an effort to hold the line on unavoidable losses, this was anathema. For these provisions were rather more expensive than those that were stocked at St. Paul and Seattle commissaries. If Paar kept this in mind, so did the stewards, who wished even more fervently that such purchases would not be needed. And none more than Bob Jones, who was planning his trip this day, or his close friend and fellow steward, Richard E. (Dick) Carlson, whose dining car Bob and his crew would relieve the following morning.

When Jones emerged from the second-floor office of Wilbur S. (Bud) Bush, assistant superintendent, with copies of the trip menus in hand, he was met by the sounds of laughter and delighted give-and-take among his crew, all of whom had gathered by the counter in the outer office. It was as though a party were in progress. Actually, it was a homecoming of sorts.

> *We looked forward to getting home, but we were just as happy to get on the road after that fourth day. You see, we had two families, really. The one at home and the one we had when we were out on the line.*
> —BOB JONES[4]

> *Well, you had a crew that was an assigned crew. The chef and the second cook and the steward, plus the*

pantry man, the linen man—the first four waiters, in fact—were all a permanent crew that were usually together for the whole trip.

—DICK CARLSON[5]

Just like a family. As Dick was saying, we worked together, ate together, lounged together—I wouldn't say slept together, but we did sleep in the same room. That was day and night for five days, wasn't it? That was more time than we had at home with our loved ones, except for vacation times. So, you see, we became very close.

—BOB JONES[6]

After greeting each other warmly, the steward and his men filed down the stairs to the first floor where, as expected, they found the commissary crew loading their supplies on four-wheeled dollies. Here Bob Jones and the first cook, or chef, remained to inventory the stock. The rest streamed single file past a counter piled high with cartons of dry staples and trooped out a door to the platform.

The car that stood before them had come in on the train from Seattle earlier that morning and had been shunted down to the coach yards from St. Paul's Union Depot. Now it was shiny-clean on the outside, and its running gear, air lines and hoses, electrical systems, air conditioning and refrigeration equipment, and other systems had been inspected and serviced by mechanical department employees. Inside, much cleaning and sanitizing were still to be done.

While others took on the pantry, the first waiter, or the pantryman—usually the waiter with the most seniority—and the third cook were responsible for kitchen floor and walls. These were stainless steel, but the floor was overlaid with cedar duckboards that helped guard against slips and falls if liquid were spilled on the metal. The men used

scalding hot water and brooms to scrub the boards while they still lay flat, then tipped them up to the walls and liberally applied more steaming water and elbow grease. For as all of them knew, methods and results were subject to intense scrutiny by minions of the U.S. Public Health Service, an agent of which was in almost constant attendance, both for inspections and to hold classes on the need for cleanliness and the means to attain and maintain it. (The Northern Pacific had been awarded the Surgeon General's Public Health Service Grade A Certificate for each operating dining car for several consecutive years.

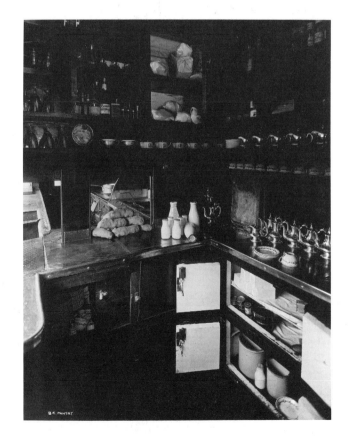

The pantry of an 1883 diner as it appeared in 1921, after having been twice remodeled

This crew was not about to mar that record.) With the car cleaned to their satisfaction, then, the cooks and waiters returned to the commissary to join the others who had begun stocking it for their trip.

On the first floor of the commissary were kept almost everything regularly used on the dining cars. There was the bake shop that made all the breads, rolls, cakes, and pastries; the butcher shop where all meats served on the cars were prepared in individual portions; two walk-in coolers for meats, dairy products, fruits, and vegetables; a walk-in freezer for vegetables, fruit, and seafood; a linen room; and a locked room where they kept all silverware. In addition, there was a kitchen where, in former times, cooks had made in advance all the soups, sauces, stocks, pie fillings, and salad dressings that were needed on the cars. At this time, it served only as a facility to prepare meals for commissary personnel and the crews who were stocking their cars.

In the basement was a gigantic walk-in cooler that could hold seven carloads of the NP's famous great big baking potatoes. Another huge storeroom held a vast array of tarnished, outdated silverware, some of it more than 70 years old. (At one time, too, according to Dick Carlson, who was assistant superintendent of dining cars for two years prior to the NP's 1970 merger into the Burlington Northern, there was a tank for keeping live lobsters, crabs, and giant Malaysian prawns. Its use was discontinued at the beginning of World War II.[7]) Much of the basement was given over to storing cases of canned goods, such as tuna, sardines, oysters, clams, fruit juices, capers, artichoke hearts, and pickled mushrooms—the sort of thing that was neither available in fresh form nor convenient to prepare even if it were.

When the crew returned after cleaning its part of the dining car, the men found dollies loaded with almost everything they would need until the train reached Seattle. For the most part, the supplies had been obtained from St. Paul provisioners. There was fresh, bottled milk from Sanitary Farm Dairies; cream purchased that day from Consumers Milk Company; half-inch pats of butter that had been churned by Land O' Lakes Creameries; bags of NP's own blend of coffee roasted by Eibert-Continental Coffee Company; a cartload of fresh, whole Minnesota walleyed pike supplied by Twin City Fish Company; cantaloupes, oranges, and tomatoes delivered just two hours earlier by Northwestern Fruit Company; beef, pork, and lamb portions cut from sides selected before dawn from racks at Armour and Swift packing plants in South St. Paul; pickled mushrooms grown and preserved by Lehmann Farms in the St. Paul suburb of Lake Elmo; individual servings of liquor stocked by McKesson and Robbins, Inc.; menus printed at Webb Publishing Company; fresh, crisp table linens and uniforms laundered by the nuns at the House of the Good Shepherd; bacon and ham from John Morrell and Company; paper-lace doilies, underliners, and finger bowl inserts from Melady Paper Company; as well as

ABOVE: Superintendent Bill Paar, center, and Carl H. Burgess, vice president for operations, accepted the U.S. Public Health Service's top award for excellence in sanitation during 1960 from Gerald W. Ferguson, right, the service's regional program director at Kansas City.
RIGHT: A commissary butcher, 1968.
OPPOSITE: Cooks and waiters stock their dining car at St. Paul, 1952.

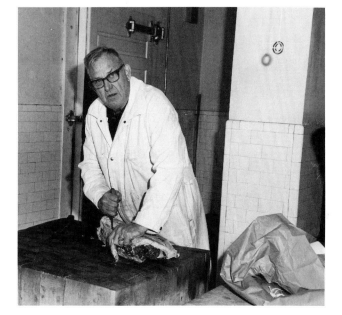

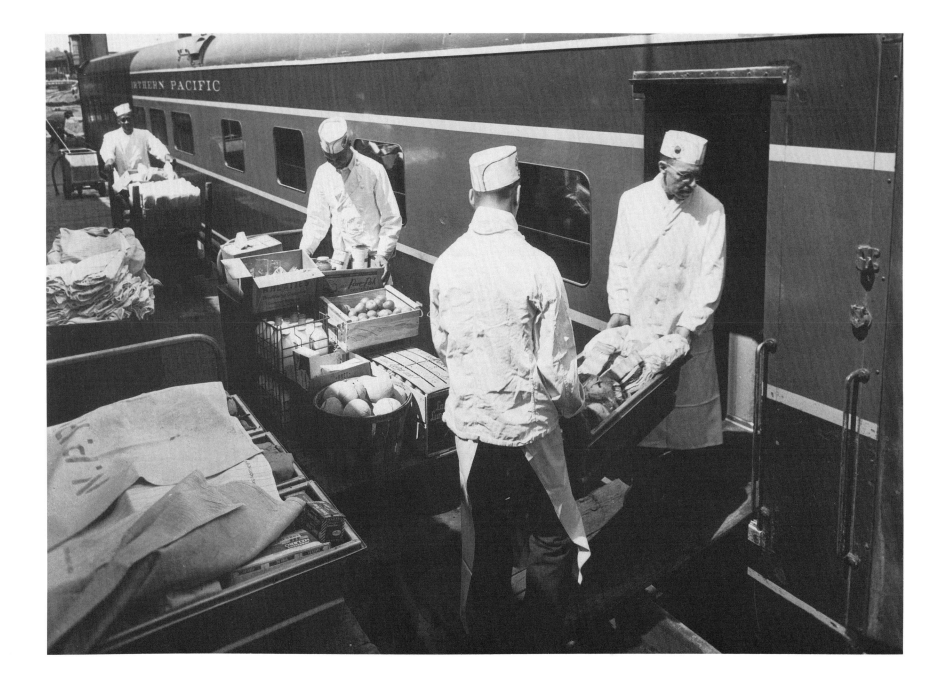

OPPOSITE: Silver storage, St. Paul commissary

toothpicks, red carnations, poultry, paper cups, flour, peanuts, soda pop, and a whole host of other items so numerous as to overwhelm the casual observer of this daily scene, who might well wonder how it all fit in the dining car.[8]

As the work of stocking began, the chef and pantryman went aboard and remained in the car to see that every item was stored in its proper place in the kitchen and pantry. All other waiters and cooks worked on the platform outside, delivering supplies from the dollies to the car in orderly fashion: baskets of oranges and melons; boxes of bread and rolls wrapped in waxed paper; sacks of potatoes; clean linens all neatly folded and ready for the linen locker; box after box and crate upon crate. Meanwhile, the housekeeping crew, all women, took over the dining area to wash down walls, windows, tiled floors, tables, and seats, after which they would vacuum the carpets throughout the car. By 2:00 P.M. the car was ready to go, and the crew members were free to return to their homes for the rest of that day, each having earned the minimum of four hours' pay, although they had worked fewer hours than that.

At 5:30 the following morning, a switch crew picked up the cleaned and stocked diner and moved it to a side track near the depot. A half-hour later, the crew arrived to board the car, change into uniforms, and start setting up for business. The No. 2 waiter, who was the designated linen man, began by placing felt pads atop the tables, followed by immaculate tablecloths, and others assisted. In the kitchen, the chef lit his gas stove and set about preparing hot cereal and half-fried bacon, while the fourth cook gathered the tools he needed at the sink to clean and fillet the walleyed pike that would be on the luncheon menu this first day out. Back in the dining area, the No. 3 waiter, who was responsible for all the silverware, deposited flatware on each table for others to set in place. Fresh long-stemmed roses were inserted in vases and a sparkling crystal and silver pitcher of water was positioned in front of the condiments on the tables. At that point, the crew felt the muffled impact of a switch engine coupling with the dining car; it sent that old thrill of anticipation through them all, for soon the car would be part of the *North Coast Limited,* and another trip would begin. It was now 6:45. The eastbound streamliner had arrived at the Union Depot five minutes earlier, after its 30-minute run from Minneapolis, and the inbound dining car had been taken off.

With the sudden thrust typical of switching operations, the car began a slow movement forward and proceeded at the same pace for two minutes, when it came to a halt. Almost as soon as it was begun, the motion was reversed and the car moved in the opposite direction. After another two minutes it was coupled with the coaches and the head end of the train, an achievement signaled by a sudden hiss from the air lines and a rattling of pipes. When this procedure was completed it was 6:51 and the aroma of freshly brewed coffee descended upon the waiters, all of whom sat in banquette sections—two booths that seated four each—at the far end of the car. As if of one mind, they slid off the benches and hurried to the kitchen, where each selected a cup. No. 1 filled them all, and they returned to their seats to savor the last break they would have for nearly three hours. For not one minute after the train began its departure from the station, about nine minutes from now, they knew the first of many breakfast patrons would be standing at the gate, waiting for the steward to admit them to his cozy, fragrant realm. Promptly at 7:00 A.M., then, the entire train was set in motion with scarcely a quiver, so smoothly did the engineer take up slack between cars and start the train rolling east and south along the river toward Dayton's Bluff and the Chicago, Burlington & Quincy yards. If all went well, as it usually did, the entire crew knew they would pass this same point on the next day just 36 hours and five minutes from now. And they would be back home to stay for four days at the end of their trip, a goal they would reach almost precisely 119 hours and 40 minutes into the future. No

one was giving any thought to that return. What mattered at the moment was the fact that they were on the road again, and that life aboard the dining car was as good as any, anywhere else.

As expected, the first guest was waiting at the gate at the very moment of departure. Bob Jones greeted him with a smile and led him to the center of the main dining section which, on the *North Coast Limited*, could seat 48 patrons. He handed the man a menu, told him he would return to take his order, and returned to his desk to greet

The third cook—called a china clipper, a pearl diver, or any of a number of names—washed the dishes.

and seat more guests. Meanwhile, a waiter came to pour a glass of water and ask the man if he would like a pot of coffee. After seating several other parties, Jones returned to take the guest's order: Oatmeal with Cream; Three-Egg Omelet with Fresh Mushrooms; Buttered Toast; Coffee. Included with this meal, which was priced at $2.15, were strawberry preserves and one of the company's popular sweet rolls, which had been prepared in the commissary bake shop the day before.[9] After the steward had written the order, he separated the paper original from its heavier manila duplicate and left the latter on the table. He would deliver the original to the chef, who received each and every check and made certain the patron's wishes were followed to the letter. Meanwhile, the waiter returned and studied his copy of the order; in fact, he did his best to memorize it on the spot.[10] He did the same at a neighboring table, and soon the car was filled with low-talking diners and darting waiters.

Today it seemed to the crew they were serving every passenger on the train, including those who had breakfasted on the other car before the train reached St. Paul. But the last guest left the car at 9:57 A.M., five minutes ahead of schedule, when the engineer whistled the station of Prairie du Chien, Wisconsin. This was fortunate, because luncheon would be served a bit earlier today to accommodate any patron who wished to eat before the train's scheduled arrival at Chicago's Union Station at 1:45 P.M. Although the kitchen crew was faced with luncheon preparations, the early departure of most of the breakfast guests gave a majority of the waiters time to eat a hurried breakfast while seated in the banquette sections at one end of the car before the last guest left the dining car. The work of sacking up soiled linen and cleaning the car for the next meal was completed and all were able to return to the dormitory car at the head end of the train to rest briefly before their own luncheon chores began.

Their quarters were in the mail-dormitory car, second in the train's consist behind the water-baggage car and three locomotive units. Thus, to reach their berths, crew members filed through the *Traveller's Rest* buffet-lounge car, two coaches, a dome coach, and a Slumbercoach (a car that provided sleeping accommodations for coach passengers). At times this trek seemed long and inconvenient, yet it was far preferable to what passed for crew quarters prior to the 1930s.[11] From September 12, 1883, until late 1929, on the *North Coast Limited,* beds were fashioned right in the dining cars by setting aside the tables and placing collapsible frames on the chairs. Rarely did this practice afford a full night's restful sleep for the men. Their beds could not be made up until the day's work was done, then had to be taken down early in the morning to permit preparations for breakfast; the train's conductors and brakemen made frequent passages through the car during the night. In fact, the dining car crew of the 1960s had few opportunities to take rest breaks during the day, such as they now enjoyed on the run to Chicago.

At 11:15 A.M. the first call for luncheon was made, a few minutes before a stop at Savanna, Illinois, where the train turned east, away from the Mississippi for the first time since it left St. Paul. It had followed the river on the Burlington Route's rail line, promoted by that company as the run "Where Nature Smiles 300 Miles." Most patrons chose to order the $3.00 table d'hôte luncheon, served in courses or on separate plates: Chicken à la Reine Soup; Broiled Minnesota Walleyed Pike; Whipped Potatoes with Butter; Green Peas au Buerre; Combination Salad with NP French Dressing; Vanilla Pudding; and Coffee (NP Special Blend). About a fourth of them selected the plate luncheon—served all on one plate—at $2.60, which featured spare ribs and sauerkraut or the pike. An even smaller number chose baked meat loaf, the alternate entrée for the table d'hôte luncheon.[12] In all, the crew served nearly 175 passengers in a matter of two hours and 15 minutes. In that time, each waiter earned some $11 in tips, a princely sum in the 1960s. When the car was empty by 1:30 P.M., the crew shifted gears.

We'd get into Chicago at 1:45, and by that time we had finished serving lunch, cleaning the car and starting to get dressed in our street clothes again to go to our hotel. Northern Pacific had agreements with hotels to house crew members overnight, using the same rooms for successive crews. There, we were on our own.

Some guys went shopping or sightseeing; some would visit friends or relatives. Others just stayed at the hotel, "pro-rated" [shared the cost] for the bottle and played cards half the night. After breakfast, we would leave the hotel about nine o'clock to go down to the car and get ready for lunch and the long run to Seattle. Depending on the passenger load, we could have a 12-hour day ahead of us. And the next day, a full one, we might go for 18 hours.

—BOB JONES[13]

The train left Chicago the next day at 12:20 P.M., and luncheon was a repetition of the inbound experience. The last customer departed as the westbound train approached Savanna and was at almost precisely the same milepost where the first luncheon guest had entered the dining car the day before. It was 2:28 P.M. and everything had gone smoothly. As usual. After all, this was an experienced crew, down to the fifth and sixth waiters, who were near the top in seniority on the extra board. (They had high hopes of moving up on the roster of regulars before the summer was out, which would almost assure them of full-time employment in the service.) Therefore, after everyone, including porters and train crew, had eaten lunch, they moved as a team to clean the car so it would be ready for dinner that evening.

As Bob Jones left to solicit dinner reservations throughout the train, the pantryman and his "mule" (waiter No. 6) accompanied by No. 3, went to the pantry to straighten it up, to note items that were in short supply, and to wipe silver and glassware with dishtowels. (As others finished their tasks, they would come to help, if necessary.) The linen man, assisted by No. 5, removed tablecloths and bagged all soiled linen from the meal. Meanwhile, No. 4 swept down and mopped the narrow, linoleum-covered hallway that ran along the wall of the car between the steward's desk and the car's vestibule. Later, after all the used linens had been bagged, he would sweep out and vacuum half the dining area. The opposite end was cleaned by No. 2.

For their part, the chef and his cooks had their hands full cleaning up in the kitchen, roasting the choice prime

For many years, soups, stocks, and large cuts of meat were prepared in steam kettles at the St. Paul commissary.

ribs that many guests would order that evening, scrubbing more than 100 pounds of the NP's famous Great Big Baked Potatoes, baking blueberry muffins and apple pies, and performing all the other kitchen chores that had to be done before the first call to dinner was made at a few minutes before 5:00 P.M. There would be little time for the crew to rest between meals today, and certainly no time to return to the dormitory car, unless one of them needed a fresh uniform.

While these tasks were being carried out, the *North Coast Limited* left Savanna and East Dubuque, Illinois, in its wake, as well as Prairie du Chien and La Crosse, Wisconsin. When the train was about 25 miles from Winona Junction, still in Wisconsin, Bob Jones went to his desk, turned on the public address system, sounded the chimes, and announced the first call to dinner. He would have a full car for both the 5:00 and 6:00 P.M. seatings, because many passengers who would detrain at St. Paul and Minneapolis wished to dine first. Arrival at St. Paul was expected at 7:05, and in Minneapolis at 7:55, both right on schedule.

The first guests ordered table d'hôte entrées. The man wanted French Onion Soup, Prime Rib, and Coffee. With this meal he received also a Relish Tray with celery, green olives, and pickled mushrooms; a Lettuce and Tomato Salad with NP French Dressing; the Great Big Baked Potato and Buttered, Fresh Asparagus; Blueberry Muffins; Natural Swiss Cheese with Toasted Crackers; and Freshly Baked Apple Pie. His wife's order was very much like his, except that she chose Grapefruit Juice as an appetizer and Broiled Frenched Lamb Chops for the entrée. The man's dinner would cost $4.15, the woman's, $3.95. A third table d'hôte entrée was Broiled Minnesota Pike, at $3.35.

The evening's menu also offered a plate dinner of Carved Turkey, Banquet Style, or the Broiled Pike, for $2.60. Usually served on a single plate, except for bread and dessert, it included a choice of two from among Au Gratin Potatoes, Peas and Carrots, and Grapefruit and

Lettuce Salad. A Dinner Roll and Rice and Raisin Custard Pudding, plus Coffee, Tea, or Milk completed the meal. In addition, for the truly hearty appetite, there was a special 16-ounce New York Cut Sirloin Steak topped with Fresh Mushroom Buttons that could be ordered with the table d'hôte dinner for $5.50.[14]

As the meal progressed through the first two calls, most of the crew members were happy to note that many of the dining car patrons were ordering prime rib. It gave them a special treat to look forward to:

> Those were 8-, 10- or 12-bone prime rib cuts. Bone and all. That's the way it was stocked on the car. And that's the way the chef would cook it, and then he would bone it. Then he would put those chine bones in the pantry hole, and that was like a dinner in itself. Because, you know, he didn't trim all the meat off. That was the sweetest part of the ribs. Anyhow, the crew loved it when we had prime ribs on the menu, because we got to eat what was left on the bones for our dinner.
>
> —Bob Jones[15]

At St. Paul, there was little slackening of dining car traffic. The train made a 25-minute stop, but there was no switching. Only the motive power was cut off and three fresh locomotive units were run in for the next leg. Two cans of garbage were handed down from the kitchen and clean replacement cans taken on. The train moved away from the depot promptly at 7:30, and Bob Jones made the third call for dinner. His first guest for this seating was the Chicago travel editor, Bill Yates, and Bob couldn't suppress a smile when the writer ordered prime rib. There surely would be enough chine bones to go around tonight.

Nearly 230 dinners had been served by the time the *North Coast Limited* reached Staples, Minnesota, at 10:05 P.M. Now, in those moments of serenity that followed a satisfyingly busy day, the banquette sections, their tables still made up, were a restful gathering place for the crew. This was especially so after they had exhausted whatever new topics of conversation may have grown out of their experiences of the past 600 miles of travel. A few of the men had drifted off to the dormitory car, but a half-dozen, joined by the train's conductor and brakeman, lingered over last cups of coffee, immersed in quiet reverie. Soon they, too, would pick their way, single file, through the still bright and lively *Traveller's Rest* car—where they would exchange cheerful greetings with the waiter-in-charge and the cook—and on through now dimly lit coaches and Slumbercoach to their own accommodations. There would be an extra hour tonight, for at the Missouri River the train would cross into the Mountain Time Zone, and that called for setting watches back one hour. Because they knew tomorrow shaped up to be the longest day of the westbound trip, all of them opted to spend that additional hour in sleep. Morning would come soon enough to all, but sooner for at least one man.

> There's an old saying among dining car crews that tells the story of what happens first thing every day on the road: "The chef is on the car to make sure the second cook calls the third cook first."
>
> —William F. Paar[16]

Well before dawn's first light, then, at about 4:30, while the train stood motionless before the depot at Dickinson, North Dakota, the third cook made his lonely trek through the dark and nearly silent cars to the kitchen. He unlocked the doors, turned on the lights, and lit the stove. From the pantry he took several sacks of NP special blend coffee, and from the refrigerator he withdrew a supply of eggs, sausage, and bacon so they could warm a bit before frying. Then he set out wrapped loaves of toasting bread and pans of sweet rolls, along with the ingredients for making muffins and griddle cakes. Now the train was rolling again, and the familiar terrain of the North Dakota

Badlands was beginning to show outside the windows as the sky lightened.

When he was satisfied that everything was ready for the chef and second cook, he set about brewing coffee, following instructions that had been drummed into him by the chef. Although the latter was responsible for making it, among the kitchen crew it was understood that a third cook could never rise to the top of his profession unless he was able to practice every procedure under working conditions. Besides, this coffee was for the crew, and a new batch would be made before the guests began to arrive for breakfast. As he stood beside the coffee maker, the door swung open and in came the chef with a smile and a hearty, "Good morning, Donny. Smells good. Just like downtown. Keep this up and you'll be as good as your dad; maybe, even, your grandfather." This was Don Welligrant, Jr., whose father had been a top chef before he became an instructor in the dining car department. And his grandfather was Joe Welligrant, a Northern Pacific master baker for some 45 years. Such savory praise would make the day seem just a little bit shorter.

The train was racing past Wibaux, 10 miles west of the North Dakota-Montana line, when the first patron entered the car at 5:51. A waiter accosted him and was about to

Train No. 25, the westbound *North Coast Limited,* headed from Minneapolis toward Staples, Minnesota, while the chef and second cook prepared four dinner entrées early in 1970.

say the car would not be open for breakfast until 6:00 A.M. when Bob Jones interrupted and showed the man to a table. After handing their guest a menu and assuring him that he would return soon for his order, Bob drew the waiter aside and asked, "Where do you get that at? This man is up early, he makes the effort to get to the dining car, so seat him and give him some coffee. You turn people away, they're going to find problems when they come back. Treat them right, and we make friends; not just for NP, but for us. Keep *that* in mind and I'll be your friend, too. What's more important, so will Mr. Paar." [17]

Some three hours after that first customer entered the car, the *North Coast Limited* had made stops at Glendive and Miles City and was about to highball out of Forsyth, Montana, where the last patron left the car. Already several waiters were eating their breakfast, and now they were joined by, not only the rest of the dining car crew, but by 12 more men and one woman, as well. These were the Pullman conductor, the Pullman porters, car attendants, and the stewardess-nurse. As a rule, the train conductor and brakeman who worked between Glendive and Billings would stop in for coffee and conversation after they had checked in any passengers who may have boarded at Forsyth. So the dining car was half-full, again.

It was the duty of No. 4 waiter to serve train personnel, but he was always assisted by No. 5 and No. 6 when those positions were filled, or by others who had finished eating earlier.[18] None expected a tip—that would be gauche—but the service they provided was no less complete than if they were serving the most generous of their regular revenue passengers. All were friends, for they often made the same run together, sharing tables at breakfast and dinner and the same hotel when they had layovers.

When the *North Coast Limited* whistled through Waco, Montana, at 9:50 A.M., the stewardess-nurse left the car amid the babble of good-natured joshing about being a tour guide. It was her duty to inform passengers, via the train's public address system, that they soon would be able to view Pompey's Pillar from the windows on the north side. This was where Capt. William Clark of the Lewis and Clark Expedition of 1804-06 had carved his signature and the date of his passage in the soft sandstone of the 200-foot-high bluff that became a popular tourist attraction. Pompey's Pillar lies some 30 miles east of Montana's largest city, Billings, where the pantryman would call ahead to Missoula for additional supplies. When he took inventory after breakfast, he decided the car would need a fresh supply of milk, cream, butter, eggs, and bacon before breakfast the next morning—a routine level of restocking during the summer travel season, when the train was running near capacity.

The NP's lunchroom in the Missoula depot was the most convenient point to restock. Although Livingston was closer, and the train would reach both stations during meal times—luncheon at Livingston, dinner at Missoula— there was much more activity at the nearer point because so many passengers detrained for trips into Yellowstone National Park. Today, at the peak of the summer travel season, the NP's station platform would be teeming with tourists, tour guides, baggage handlers, and cab and bus drivers, not to mention a small army of NP train and passenger personnel. It was not a place to be cast adrift with a cartload of perishables. When the pickup was made at Missoula that evening, it was completed without a hitch on a platform almost devoid of passengers.

At 10:00 P.M. that night, while the entire crew and their usual "company" were gathered in the dining car— only the train conductor and brakeman differed from those who had joined them a night earlier—they passed the halfway point: 2,318 miles covered. The train was four miles east of Rathdrum, Idaho. It had taken 65 hours to reach that mark, and they would be back at their home terminal, St. Paul, in 59 hours. The work of handling half the 14 meals of their round trip was heavy, when compared with other times of the year when travel was lighter, but not one of them would say they had never worked harder or longer. In fact, with the two special tour parties going east with them tomorrow, there might be more than 50 more to feed.

When the speeding *North Coast Limited* crossed the invisible line between Idaho and Washington at 10:17 P.M., the train conductor and brakeman left the dining car. They would detrain at Spokane, where a new train crew would take over. Car attendants, porters, and the Pullman conductor departed, also, to be ready for passengers who would board at this gateway city to the Inland Empire. Meanwhile, instead of retiring to their dormitory on wheels, the dining car crewmen stationed themselves along the south side of the train, seated beside the car's picture windows. They were hoping to catch a glimpse of friends among the crew on the eastbound *North Coast Limited*, which had left Seattle at 1:30 that afternoon. In Spokane, during the summer travel season from early June to mid-September, the two streamliners would sit at the station together for nearly 15 minutes with only a platform separating them, and the crews could communicate by sign language. During the rest of the year, the westbound *North Coast Limited* would arrive here an hour later, and all the other meetings took place during meal times or while crews were asleep.

Both trains departed at exactly 10:45, one going west toward the Columbia Basin and the Cascade Mountains, the other east and into the remote reaches of the northern Rocky Mountains. Only then did the cooks and waiters repair to their beds. All felt they had earned a full night's sleep, but a few light sleepers were not expecting to get it. Because at 1:36 A.M., the train arrived at Pasco, Washington, where a Vista-Dome coach and sleeping car No. 253 were switched out of the train and coupled to the Spokane, Portland and Seattle Railway Company's train No. 1, which followed the Columbia River to Portland. (The two cars were owned by the SP&S, whose capital stock and

bonds were owned, 50 percent each, by the Northern Pacific and Great Northern railways.) At 2:01, the *North Coast Limited* got underway again, quite undetected by any member of the dining car crew, all of whom—including those who had expected to be awakened by those switching operations in Pasco—were lost in honest slumber until the train had passed Yakima and was more than 120 miles west of Pasco. Then, at the appointed hour, the third cook left the dormitory to perform his prebreakfast chores some minutes before they reached Ellensburg. This morning he was joined only a few minutes later by the chef and the pantryman, both of whom had to check over their supplies and prepare orders for restocking in Seattle. But first, the streamliner would have to climb up to the two-mile-long Stampede Tunnel, which breached the Cascade Range at an altitude of 2,852 feet.[19]

At Ellensburg, the rails lay at an elevation of 1,510 feet. Thus, in the 51 miles from there to the tunnel, the track would rise by more than one-quarter of a mile. In the 51 miles beyond the west portal of the tunnel, the train would run down 2,764 feet, or more than a half-mile, to a mere 88 feet above sea level at East Auburn. The elapsed time for that section of track was two hours and 30 minutes, at an average speed of just over 40 miles per hour. By the time the *North Coast Limited* left Auburn at 7:35, most of the passengers who had wished to dine before their scheduled arrival at Seattle (8:15 A.M.), had returned to their coach seats or sleeper space. Then, as the train rolled slowly past the NP's commissary on its way into the station, the crew's order books were tossed out the door to a waiting clerk. And when all movement had ceased, the steward, the chef, and the waiter-in-charge of the *Traveller's Rest* car alighted from the train and rode back to the commissary to exchange soiled linens for a clean supply and to help get their orders together.

After all passengers had detrained, a yard engineer took over the controls in the first diesel locomotive unit and backed the train to a wye, turned it, and slowly ran the

whole thing through an automatic washer. Later, while the train was being inspected and serviced, commissary personnel delivered those new supplies to the yard, about six blocks away. There the crew restocked the car and the train was backed down beside the station platform, well ahead of its scheduled 1:30 P.M. departure. Crew members enjoyed no rest break, however, other than a chance to stretch their legs during a brief stroll about the depot. Despite the train's afternoon departure, lunch would be served at the start of the eastbound trip out of Seattle. Therefore, the car had to be cleaned, its tables set, and cooking begun in the kitchen.

By the time they revisited Ellensburg, going in the opposite direction, not quite 12 hours had elapsed, and Bob Jones had just completed a hurried trip through the train to make dinner reservations. The train was now in the Kittitas Valley, where the Great Big Baked Potato had been discovered by Superintendent Hazen J. Titus in 1909, and the steward and waiters were ready to greet the first guest for dinner.

There were not many additional mouths to feed this evening. The Rainier Park directors and their wives had come aboard at East Auburn, following their trip from Tacoma on a Northern Pacific Transport Company bus,

The chef fries eggs on a *Mainstreeter* buffet dining car.

but they were only 14 in number. A better test of the department's longtime slogan, "Famously Good Food," awaited the crew the next day. The large number of coach passengers would be swelled by the party of 44 teenagers and chaperones from Portland, whose car the train would pick up in Pasco about 7:35 A.M. Most of them patronized the SP&S diner for dinner, so the pressure would come during the rest of the trip into St. Paul. That is, if there were to be much added pressure. From long experience, the dining car crewmen knew that young people often preferred the menu and service offered in the *Traveller's Rest* car. However, it was likely that many of them had never eaten in a diner before and might well test the waters at breakfast and dinner the following day.

As it turned out, they ate breakfast as a group—virtually filling the dining car—after the train had climbed over Homestake Pass (6,356 feet), the highest point en route, west of Butte, Montana. At lunch and dinner the student group could not be accommodated en masse, even though they dined late at both meals, so Bob Jones kept all their checks together and settled up with the leader after everyone was certain all had been served. This meant, of course, that it had been one of the dreaded 18-hour days.

All in the crew conceded, however, that the youths had been unusually well behaved and so undemanding that it actually had been rather enjoyable to serve them. Besides, because this had been an organized passenger movement, gratuities had been added to the lump-sum settlements on a percentage basis and then prorated among the crew. All in all, a most satisfactory outcome of a very long day.

> *We didn't make much more than the minimum wage, even under our union contract. But we compensated by making tips. With those, we made money. Not every passenger was a good tipper. But, you know, the next two are going to tip you. You realized that some of them just didn't have it to give you. But you gave them the same kind of service you gave everybody. That was instilled in us. I know a few waiters would kind of give them a bad time, but most of us knew we'd have our money when we got to St. Paul.*
> —BOB JONES[20]

When the crew trooped ahead to the dormitory car after midnight, with only a trace of weariness in their actions, little thought was given to the fact that they would get less

Younger patrons received special menus.

than five hours' sleep this night. Already the *North Coast Limited* was approaching Valley City, North Dakota, and in just over an hour it would cross the Red River of the North into Minnesota. Breakfast would be served as usual, but because the dining car would be cut off when it reached St. Paul, there was no way everyone could be served. Therefore, late in the evening, the steward had switched on the intercom and made an announcement:

May I have your attention, please? This is your steward, Robert Jones. I must tell you that tomorrow morning, when we reach St. Paul, the dining car will be taken off this train and a fresh one put on. We appreciate that this will be inconvenient for some of you, and for this we are sorry. However, this car will be open for business at 5:30 A.M., and we will be serving breakfast until 6:40. For those of you who

The Big Baked Potato shared a display with children's menus featuring denizens of Yellowstone National Park in the window of the NP's New York ticket office on Fifth Avenue, 1926.

have destinations between St. Paul and Chicago, I am happy to say that the fresh diner will begin serving at the moment the train leaves the St. Paul Union Depot. I want you to know we have had a pleasant trip with you, and I hope we will have the pleasure of traveling with you again in the future. Thank you, and good night.[21]

The crew repeated its morning routine, and the train soon arrived in St. Paul. The diner was replaced with a fresh one, and the crew rode its car behind the switch engine across the yard to the commissary, where the car once again was shunted in beside the platform. It was now their duty to "unstock" the car, performing in reverse the work they had done six days earlier. In addition, each item was counted and the totals entered on NP Form 9064, Supply Report. ("This report must be properly filled out and delivered to the Superintendent Dining Cars at the terminus of the trip, immediately after taking a complete inventory of All Supplies and Equipment."[22]) When these instructions were followed, the form revealed everything that had been stocked before the trip, the amount and source of any supplies obtained while en route, the total goods on hand at the end of the trip, and the amount consumed. Inside the front cover there was space to note supplies that may have been condemned, date of condemnation, and their value.

Taking the completed form, along with all his meal checks and trip receipts of nearly $9,000, Bob Jones reported to the bookkeeping section on the second floor and entered the office of Harvey Roloff, department accountant.

"Good morning, Robert. Have a good trip? Oh, just put that stuff on the desk. I'm sure you want to get home as soon as you can. I'll check through it later. Anyhow, you keep your books in better shape than any of them, so I know everything's all right. Give my best to your wife. We'll see you in a few days."[23]

Outside the walls of this building, where so many people entered, worked, and departed, where food enough to feed armies was stored and cooked and issued over four decades, the clouds again floated in suspended relief against a blue sky, and an empty dining car awaited an engine that would shunt it several hundred feet to a spot where it would undergo a routine but minute inspection. It stood there now, inert, silent, almost barren, not at all the picture of elegance on wheels that, for five days, had inspired anticipation and delight and wonder in more than 500 travelers, few of whom appreciated what a marvel of efficiency it was, or how unique was its place in the history of travel. To those few who understand how enormously important was its contribution, it stands at the pinnacle, unchallenged even by all those modern cruise ships that ply the seven seas. Where else, the knowing ones may ask, can one find that joyous combination of movement toward a goal, food in a pleasing variety, ineffably delightful scenery, service fit for a reigning monarch, and a feeling of intimacy that is totally at odds with time and place? And they will tell you that the dining car is more than a triumph, it is the logical ending for a search that had its genesis countless millennia in the past.

Eating on the Road

E ATING HAS BEEN A MAJOR CONCERN of travelers almost since time began, especially when trips were of some distance and duration. The kinds of food chosen and the amount of time required to eat them have been tied closely to progress in modes of transportation and in methods of food preservation and preparation. For millennia before the first rustic inn was founded, travelers either carried provisions or ate off the land. In fact, the earliest inns offered little more than a roof over the heads of their patrons. The stopping place where Jacob's sons rested on their return from Egypt, as told in Genesis, afforded them only that much; Reuben and his brothers had to furnish their own food and bedding, as well as fodder for their animals. At last, on some unrecorded red-letter day during the Middle Ages, some enterprising innkeeper offered to a weary wayfarer a home-cooked meal from his own table— the table d'hôte—and invented the restaurant.[1]

At the Tabard Inn, celebrated by Chaucer in his *Canterbury Tales* before 1400, a complete table d'hôte meal, including wine or ale, could be had for a price. But among the 30-odd excursionists on that pilgrimage, a group of five businessmen had engaged a cook to accompany them. His presence would seem to tell us that not all of the inns they would patronize during the 60-mile, six-day trek on horseback were set up to provide meal service. This feature of hostels and inns was slow to evolve until innholders recognized it as a means to increase business and enhance their income. It had become almost de rigueur by 1600, apparently, when a whole body of laws governed the innkeeping profession. One regulation, dating from the 17th century, noted that "it must not be accounted a small matter to afford house room, lodging, rest and food to the comfort of God's children." And an act of the English parliament in 1604 declared that "the ancient, true and proper use of Inns, Alehouses and Victualling Houses was for the Receipt, Relief and Lodging of Wayfaring People traveling from Place to Place . . . and not meant for the entertainment and harbouring of Lewd

and Idle People to spend and consume their Money and Time in Lewd and Drunken Manner."[2]

By this time, also, another important advance in travelers' gustatory odyssey was on the immediate horizon. Before the midpoint of the 17th century, the stagecoach made its debut as a public conveyance, and many inns began serving as stage depots and terminals; in fact, new ones were erected with this convenience in mind. When they were built with waiting rooms, ticket windows, and separate "gates" for coaches departing in different directions, these foreshadowed the modern railroad station. The numbers of such establishments declined as the distance a coach could cover in a day increased from about 15 to 40 miles, weather and road conditions permitting. But many more were to close with the coming of railroad passenger service. A train powered by an iron horse more than doubled the best daily mileage effort of the coach-and-four it replaced.

The innkeepers continued to feed people on the move, however, and engine drivers still halted for the obligatory 20 minutes, just as horse drivers had done. The only real change dealt with ownership of the inns themselves; railroad builders got into the act after 1838, either building facilities or contracting with caterers to provision the passengers. The canny caterers to the Great Western Railway of London wrote into their contract a provision that the firm's trains could never stop at Swindon station, Wiltshire, without a layover of at least 20 minutes.[3]

Even in the United States the railroads had avoided looking for ways to better the lot of the hungry passenger. American railroad managers thought of themselves as people movers, not caterers. Impelled by the electric prod of competition, they devoted their energies and financial resources to obtaining better coaches and sleeping cars than others in the field.

The first coaches looked for all the world like stagecoaches mounted on flanged wheels. But, of course, the craftsmen were the same people who had been turning out

OVERLEAF: A *North Coast Limited* dining car, 1934. A few of the "diners" were professional models, but most were NP employees from the company's St. Paul general offices, who received $1.00 and signed a release permitting the company to use the photograph in its advertising.

rolling stock for the coaching lines. The genius at the Baltimore and Ohio Railroad who, in 1835, brought us the first passenger car designed with seats on both sides of a center aisle, providing access and egress at its ends instead of the sides, and mounted on eight wheels rather than four, established a pattern that is essentially still in use. This early example of Yankee ingenuity applied to railroading was also more in keeping with the principles of a representative democracy. Heteronomous England clung for decades to compartmentalized cars fitted with coaching-style side doors.[4]

The old coaching inn idea of meal stops continued to dominate, although complaints about the food and service, often accompanied by proposals for ways to improve them, flitted through newspaper and magazine accounts of adventuresome trips on the new but perilous mode of transportation. Ocean liners, river steamers, and canal boats were suggested as role models for food service, of course, and a rail car built in 1835 for the Philadelphia and Columbia Railroad boasted what must have been a food service counter at one end, an innovation that withered as railroad executives concentrated their efforts on haulage to the exclusion of forage. In the early 1860s, cars that were used to provide meals were nothing more than temporary expedients: the sheds on wheels used for construction crews, stripped-down baggage cars, coaches remodeled into lunch-counter cars. Some coaches were only half-gutted and fitted out with counters, thus serving as forerunners to the coffee shop/coach cars on "milk-stop" runs that were little patronized by those who demanded luxury as a birthright.

All these were merely stopgaps to forestall the inevitable and were adopted, usually, by railroads that felt the pinch of competition. As a result, little thought was given to dining comfort or variety, and only patrons who could not wait for an end to their journeys, or who did not expect anything better, patronized them. It was not surprising, therefore, that there was no stampede to provide or improve a service that was shunned by a majority of passengers, as well as by one's rivals. So the impasse continued, and it became a game of watchful waiting.

Rumors of better things persisted among passengers, but nothing of substance emerged to support them until George Mortimer Pullman came to grips with the problem.[5]

It could be said that Pullman entered the business world as a "sergeant of industry," for he began his career as a cabinetmaker in Chicago shortly after 1850. Nine years later he joined forces with railroad builder Benjamin Field and began converting passenger coaches into sleeping cars for the Chicago and Alton Railroad. Soon, Field and his partner were buying sleeping cars from other makers and contracting with midwestern railroads to run them over those lines. By 1865 they had contracted with seven Chicago-based railroads, among which were the Michigan Central, Chicago and North-western, and the Chicago, Burlington & Quincy (variously known as the Burlington, the CB&Q, and the Q). Pullman was aware of the opportunities the new transcontinentals would present for builders of sleeping cars, and he was ready to strike out on his own.

He severed his ties with Field in 1866 and formed the Pullman Palace Car Company. Within a few months he was casting about for a solution to the dual problem of providing both sleeping accommodations and food service in a single car. The result was his widely heralded hotel car, far and away the best idea to hit the industry since its birth, especially for the more affluent. Here was a car providing comfortable seats by day that could be converted to beds by night; it included a miniature kitchen, where a chef could conjure up meals fit for the world's nobility. It was also an expensive unit affordable only to a few well-financed railroads whose routes were also long enough to make such equipment a virtual necessity.

With the introduction of his hotel car in 1867, Pullman's dream of creating a fleet of cars that bespoke

luxury in every respect had been realized. But passengers, who should have been overjoyed at their good fortune, were nothing if not inconsistent. They now whined about cooking aromas that pervaded their cars day and night. Pullman's response was to move his kitchens from the center of the cars to one end and to install rudimentary exhaust systems that drew offensive odors through the roof as the cars whizzed along the rails. In 1869 the Union Pacific Railroad contracted for several of these cars and ran a well-advertised "Hotel Train." Then, early in 1870, when it became apparent the car was a money-loser, the company backed down and reverted to its meal stops.

Other railroad managers were also unconvinced that the investment was worth it. Concerned directors, and the shareholders who elected them, both watched the bottom line. The problems were as simple as the rules of supply and demand. Nearly as large a crew was needed for a single car as that required to operate the rest of the train, and meal prices offended all but the affluent. Who could afford to pay 50 to 60 cents for a meal of only meat and potatoes, plus 25 cents for tea or coffee? Those who could were just as likely to order a table d'hôte spread for $1.00, plus the tab for wine or champagne. As a consequence, rarely more than 10 passengers beyond the car's capacity of 30 took advantage of the service. On a cost-plus-profit basis—the railroad guaranteeing to cover costs and provide a negoti-ated profit, no matter what the income—only Pullman stood to gain. When he realized this, he set about conjur-ing up another solution to the problem, and soon devel-oped and introduced a car devoted exclusively to meal service, his restaurant car. And he linked operations with construction (an approach that served his company well until trustbusters intruded and ordered divestiture).

In 1868 he unveiled a truly magnificent vehicle and changed the world of dining-in-transit for all time. It was the dining car *Delmonico*, progenitor of a line that survived with little change until the mid-1970s, when Amtrak in-troduced a bilevel diner that reflected economic and

political realities to a degree undreamed of in Pullman's day. Keeping faith with his vision of grandeur and sensual elegance for the wealthy hedonists who traveled wherever tracks were laid, Pullman produced a car that cost $20,000, nearly twice the cost of a steam locomotive. At 60 feet long by 10 feet wide, it matched the dimensions of his hotel car, but the kitchen area was more than doubled. Oddly enough, it was in the car's mid-section, a good indication that he did not think his patrons would object to aromas wafting from it at mealtime, just as long as they were not expected to endure them 24 hours a day. For some passengers, particularly the keen-scented and those prone to motion sickness, that was the beauty of it; they could enjoy a meal, then repair to their parlor cars and sleepers, redolent *only* of locomotive fumes, prolonged human occupation, toilet waters, an admixture of the latest Paris essences and, occasionally, the unconcealable odor of an illicit after-dinner cigar.

The *Delmonico* accommodated up to 48 diners at a single sitting, 24 on either side of the kitchen. This was more than half again as many as the hotel car handled at one time. A crew of six—two cooks and four waiters—could serve as many as 250 meals each day, instead of the 120 their predecessors had managed. With the larger kitchen, the increased staff could also produce longer, more varied menus with a greater price range, allowing a much broader segment of the traveling public to avail itself of service.

Despite the restaurant car's almost immediate accept-ance among passengers, however, rail managements acted almost in concert, but tacitly, to ignore the pride of the Pullman works. Obviously, their aversion to red ink could not be overcome by creating increased opportunities to use it. The norm was a widely shared hope that the whole idea of en-route meals would go away and rid the rails of a financially debilitating experiment. But wishing would not make it so. Passengers grew even more demanding, and maverick lines persisted in serving meals as a means to lure

OPPOSITE: The 22-room Highland House at Hope, Idaho Territory, was built by the NP for sportsmen at a cost of $4,000 in 1886.

patronage away from their competition. Whenever one opportunistic management caved in to popular demand, another felt compelled to respond in kind and hang the expense. Thus, collusive agreements and the illusion of coexistence collapsed beneath the weight of self-interest.

Yet the *Delmonico* was not cut out to be an orphan. After test runs on several roads operating between Chicago and New York, as well as in the Chicago area, the car was leased by the Chicago and Alton. Operated by Pullman on a cost-plus-profit basis, it ran on C&A trains between the lakefront metropolis and Kansas City. As a consequence, westbound travelers flocked to the C&A station's gates, much to the dismay of the CB&Q; the Chicago, Rock Island, and Pacific; the Toledo, Wabash, and Western; and the Atchison, Topeka, and Santa Fe railroads, which earlier had enjoyed greater patronage than their smaller competitor. Faced with declining revenues, they were compelled to match the service, and Pullman, at long last, could revel in the prospect of good fortune, even if it came at the expense of reluctant railroads.

Savoring its success, the Chicago and Alton kept the pressure on, gradually increasing its fleet until, by 1872, it had signed up for five of Pullman's diners. Within a decade, after virtually all Chicago-based, long-haul railroads had entered the contest, this brash (some thought rash) trend-setter purchased the cars and created a new model of procedure by operating them in house. More-over, it reduced the price of table d'hôte meals from Pullman's standard of $1.00 to an unheard-of 75 cents. This invited even commoners to choose the C&A as their preferred route, with the result that dining cars suddenly were commonplace in the Midwest. The roads in the East could no longer resist the movement. But even as the Baltimore and Ohio put the first hole in the eastern boycott in 1881, the western lines grew more obstinate in their efforts to exclude dining cars.

Collusive disbarment of restaurants-on-rails had been discussed among all the railroads, but in the West, where only three trunk lines controlled all the long-haul passenger business, rhetoric was converted to action. Presidents of the Santa Fe, the Burlington, and the Union Pacific shared the opinion that adding dining cars would have no long-term effect on passenger traffic. If one line did something foolish, its increase in travelers would be only temporary, for the other two would simply follow suit and restore the original balance. Then all of them would be saddled with what everybody knew was an unnecessary financial burden. Besides, hadn't each invested heavily in station restaurants? Accordingly, on November 21, 1881, representatives of the three companies executed this terse, unequivocal agreement:

> *It is hereby agreed by and between the Chicago Burlington and Quincy Railroad Company, the Atchison Topeka and Santa Fe Railroad Company, and the Union Pacific Railway Company, that neither party to this agreement shall run regularly on its trains between the Missouri River and Denver any Dining or Hotel cars, without first giving the other parties hereto written notice of intention to do so, at least six (6) months in advance of so doing.*
> Chicago Burlington and Quincy R. R. Co.
> By T. J. Potter, General Manager
> Atchison Topeka and Santa Fe R. R. Co.
> By C. B. Wheeler, General Manager
> Union Pacific Railway Co.
> By Thos. L. Kimball
> Asst. Genl. Manager[6]

All remained peaceful in this rail baron's Eden until a gnat of the far north was seen to be something much more than a pesky, ineffectual nuisance. The Northern Pacific Railroad Company—the NP—completed its transcontinental line between Duluth and Portland on August 22, 1883, and inaugurated regular, daily passenger service, including dining cars, on September 12. Neither the UP nor the Santa Fe paid it much mind. After all, the newcomer had yet to prove itself, and there was every reason to believe it would founder. Meanwhile, a few clouds glowered briefly on their own horizons, but no storm materialized. In 1884, George W. Holdrege, assistant general manager for the CB&Q, wrote to Thomas L. Kimball, his opposite at the UP, that the Burlington would withdraw from the agreement six months later, on November 10, 1884. No reason was given, and the CB&Q made no move to add diners to its Denver trains. In 1886, the UP also withdrew, but continued to honor the agreement. The most unsettling crisis arose in 1887, when the UP's passenger department personnel awoke to a sharp decline in their first-class passenger business.

At first it had been seen as a momentary fluctuation, nothing to be concerned about. But the trickle became a flood and, according to a UP historian, the NP's use of dining cars in its trains to the Pacific Coast "resulted in such an increase in the number of its first class passengers, and such a decrease to the Union Pacific, to the same competitive territory, that the passenger department officers urgently advised that the Union Pacific follow the Northern Pacific's lead."[7]

The situation was further compounded in the following year when the Rock Island completed its line to Denver and soon advertised use of "through vestibule passenger trains, with dining cars included in their consists, between Chicago and Denver." By 1889 the UP's top management could not ignore the loss of business to the upstart NP and Rock Island. Despite protests by the CB&Q and Rock Island, the UP initiated full dining car service just before the new year of 1890. With the installation of dining cars on the Santa Fe line in 1891, all western transcontinentals offered a full range of choices for their passengers, thanks to Henry Villard and the Northern Pacific. How could this have happened?

Building the
Northern Pacific

I T MIGHT BE SAID THAT the Northern Pacific Railroad was, from the outset, a manifestation of a familiar New Testament warning: The first shall be last, and the last shall be first. For, although it was the last of the federally chartered transcontinentals to place a last crosstie, line a last rail, and drive a last spike, it was a vision in the minds of men even before railroads were invented. It might even be said to have been first imagined by Thomas Jefferson.[1]

The dream of opening the Pacific Northwest to settlement and commerce with the East is not much younger than the vision of a free and united nation of American states. That both ideas were largely shaped in the mind of Jefferson should surprise no one. Yet the Northern Pacific's debt to him goes well beyond this. While a member of Congress in 1784, he drafted an ordinance for the new Northwest Territory, that vast unsettled region between the Appalachians and the Mississippi, northwest of the Ohio River. The provisions of this document were included in modified form in the Ordinance of 1785, as well as in the familiar Northwest Ordinance of 1787. And from the 1785 ordinance came the principle of the federal land grant: one section of land in each township was to be set aside for public school maintenance. Too, it was during Jefferson's later presidency that Congress first stipulated that a percentage of the proceeds from the sale of public lands would be granted to new states for use in building roads. In a very real sense, this legislation introduced the idea of federal aid to transportation and paved the way for railroad land grants in the 19th century.

The first practical steam locomotive was still more than a half-century away, but "communication"— transportation—was uppermost in Jefferson's thoughts: he envisioned a cross-country riverway as the most likely means of linking East with West, utilizing the Mississippi and Missouri rivers as the main lines of communication. Jefferson saw to that when on May 14, 1804, Captains Meriwether Lewis and William Clark set forth "to trace the Missouri to its source, to cross the Highlands, and

follow the best water communication which offered thence to the Pacific Ocean." When Lewis and Clark returned to St. Louis on September 23, 1806, the news of their triumph spread across the United States and Europe. Their expedition laid to rest, as Alexander Mackenzie had done earlier in Canada, any hope that the Creator had somehow managed to endow this most favored of lands with such a facile transcontinental passage. But their descriptions of the new lands led to an almost immediate acceleration in the pace of both westward migration and visionary speculation on the extension of commerce and trade beyond the western banks of the Mississippi.

In the years that followed, several men were to promote the idea of rail transportation between the Atlantic and the Pacific. Robert Mills, an architect and engineer from South Carolina, claimed that in 1819 he had been the first to propose a rail connection between the headwaters of navigable rivers running to each ocean. Soon after 1830, when the first functional railroad was built in the East, Dr. Samuel B. Barlow, a physician from Granville, Massachusetts, urged the Congress to build a road from New York to the mouth of the Columbia "in about 46 degrees N. Lat." His ideas were expressed in letters to newspaper editors as far west as Michigan from about 1833 to 1844, when the mantle of advocacy fell to Asa Whitney, a disciple of greater volubility and persistence.[2]

Whitney, who had amassed a small fortune from foreign trade as a merchant in China, saw the advantages such a road would bring for trade with Asia. He undertook an extensive but unsuccessful personal crusade that lasted more than a quarter of a century. In the 1850s he was joined by Edwin F. Johnson, a capitalist, educator, civil engineer—one of the most highly regarded of his day—and builder of railroads, the man who would become the first chief engineer of the Northern Pacific Railroad. Johnson's reasoned arguments for a northern route won serious attention, but the more divisive issues of slavery and states' rights, as well as the demands of gold seekers in California,

OVERLEAF: NP crew laying rails, about 1870

brought suggestions for alternate lines. When Secretary of War Jefferson Davis, a champion of Southern rights and expansion of slave territory, took the problem in hand in 1853, the solution was perhaps foreordained. He recommended building the southernmost of five proposed lines, roughly tracing the 32nd parallel through Texas and the Territory of New Mexico. Opposition from all other sections of the country was immediate as well as fatal to a prompt resolution of the raging debate. Before any compromise could be reached, the War between the States broke out, and it was not until 1862 that Congress opted for the middle route, that of the Union Pacific. This magnanimous but futile gesture fairly bellowed of President Abraham Lincoln's sincere desire for peace and unity, but the war was to last three more years. During that time,

Congress thought it prudent to locate a second line that would be beyond the reach of Confederate forces. Therefore, on July 2, 1864, President Lincoln signed a charter authorizing construction of the Northern Pacific Railroad from Lake Superior to Puget Sound.[3]

As Lincoln dotted the i in his signature on the Northern Pacific's charter, unbridled euphoria gripped the heirs of Jefferson's dream. But their enthusiasm was soon dampened, for Congress had provided little to ensure success for the project. The first Pacific Railroad and Telegraph Act had been a veritable Christmas tree, splendidly decorated with large land grants, government bonds, and indulgent loans with easy payment plans. Still smarting from widespread criticism aroused by their generosity, the national legislature armed itself against any

NP survey crew, Cold Spring, Minnesota, July 1869

charge of largess in approving the northern route bill. The NP charter, although blessed with a double portion of land, was denied both money *and* the right to mortgage the land as a means of raising funds for construction. As a result, no construction funds could be raised.[4]

Perhaps realizing its error, Congress approved an amendment to the railroad's charter in March 1869 that allowed the company to issue bonds for construction backed by a mortgage on its railroad and telegraph line; an amendment passed the next year, after heated debate, permitted the company to issue bonds backed by the land

grant. Early in 1870, New York financier Jay Cooke took on the task of marketing NP construction bonds. He managed to raise about $5 million by February 1, 1870, and the great work was underway.[5]

To satisfy a congressional mandate for the start of construction, a groundbreaking ceremony was staged in the frozen reaches of a northern Minnesota forest on February 15. The hoary domain of deer and bear and otter and beaver was invaded by a mixed group of movers and shakers from Minnesota and Wisconsin, artfully chosen by Jay Cooke, who was soon to purchase all the land between

Groundbreaking, Minnesota Junction, 1870

this point and Lake Superior. Shovels could not dent the rock-hard earth, so the celebrants gathered on the edge of Otter Creek, where a small bonfire was built to soften the soil. Afterward, a few scourings of snowy sand were placed in a wheelbarrow by the mayors of Duluth (Joshua B. Culver) and Superior (Hiram Hayes) and rousing cheers rent the air. The 85-year-old dream of crossing the continent was on the brink of reality. All that remained was 13 more years of conglomerated ecstasy and despair.[6]

A contract to build the Minnesota Division was let in June, and grading was begun in July. In advance of the roadbed's clamshells, engineers moved westward, staking out a definite location for the line. On their heels, driving horse and buggy, rode Thomas H. Canfield, a Vermont capitalist who had built the Chicago, St. Paul, and Fond du Lac Railroad, picking sites for towns and stations. As president of the Lake Superior and Puget Sound Company, a townsite ingroup formed outside the railroad by several of its officers and directors, he laid out, in east-to-west procession, the future Gopher State communities of Kimberly, Aitkin, Brainerd, Motley, Aldrich, Wadena, Perham, Audubon, Lake Park, Hawley, Glyndon, and Moorhead. The board of directors singled out Brainerd as the NP's operating headquarters. Here, too, would be the company's principal shops, a colonist reception house for emigrants, and the Headquarters Hotel. The manager of the hotel restaurant could boast that it was the NP's first permanent dining facility established for the comfort and convenience of rail passengers. Employees lived in and ate at the second building erected in Brainerd, a boarding-house built for them.[7]

Meanwhile, work moved ahead more rapidly on the North Pacific Coast. After selecting the site for Moorhead, Canfield went west to Washington Territory, where the milder climate had enabled the NP's construction department to initiate grading by company forces much earlier than in Minnesota. When Canfield arrived, 25 miles had been graded north from Kalama on the

Columbia River, but no rails had been laid, because they had to be shipped around the Horn of South America. The Lake Superior & Puget Sound Company's well-traveled president located Tenino, Newaukem, Olequa, and Kalama, Washington, but at Kalama it was merely a formality: two dozen buildings occupied the site when he arrived. Aside from blessing the engineers' choice, his principal contribution at Kalama was a hotel and restaurant, which he named Kazano House after a local Indian leader. Its owner was the townsite company, not the railroad, but NP passengers would later patronize the restaurant. Although it was completed during February 1871, before the NP's Headquarters Hotel at Brainerd, it must take second place in the railroad's dining facility chronology, for tracklaying began at Kalama after April 29, 1871, by which time the Minnesota city already had at least a modicum of train service.

Tracklaying continued across Minnesota, reaching the site selected for Moorhead on the North Dakota border on December 30, 1871. Fargo, across the Red River, was the site of the railroad's second meal stop on the east end of its route. A boardinghouse was built there during the summer of 1872 to board Gen. Thomas L. Rosser and his staff of engineers, NP division personnel, army officers, contractors, and transients in town on railroad business.

But when the first passenger train arrived on June 8, 1872, a mixed complement of excursionists and immigrants were glad to be served a meal in an employee boarding car, a gabled-roof structure surmounting a flat car. Many of these would soon become stand-ins for more sophisticated facilities when the Northern Pacific's fortunes fell on hard times. The service they afforded was colorfully described in the memoirs of Elizabeth B. Custer, wife of western military history's goat (or hero, depending on one's sympathies), Lt. Col. George Armstrong Custer. Custer and the Seventh Cavalry had been assigned to the newly established Fort Abraham Lincoln, five miles south of Bismarck on the west bank of the Missouri, early in April

Headquarters Hotel, Brainerd

1873. In the summer of 1874, permanent quarters were nearly completed. Custer went to Michigan and returned with his Libbie. Her 1885 account of the trip is replete with references to the food service they had encountered en route:

> After long debates with her parents, we had captured a young lady who was to return with us. She was a "joy forever," and submitted without a word to the rough part of our journey. After we left St. Paul, the usual struggle for decent food began. Some of the officers returning from leave of absence had joined us, and we made as merry over our hardships as we could. When we entered the eating-houses, one young member of our party, whom we called the "butter fiend," was made the experimenter. If he found the butter too rancid to eat undisguised, he gave us a hint by saying, under his breath, "this is a double-over place." That meant that we must put a layer of bread on top of the butter to smother the taste.
>
> The general was so sensitive when living in civilization that the heartiest appetite would desert him if an allusion to anything unpleasant or a reference to suffering was made at the table. But he never seemed to be conscious of surroundings when "roughing it." Of course I had learned to harden myself to almost anything by this time, but I can see the wide-open eyes of our girl friend when she saw us eat all around any foreign ingredients we found in our food. She nearly starved on a diet consisting of the interior of badly-baked potatoes and the inside of soggy rolls.
>
> One of the eating-places on the road was kept in a narrow little house, built on a flat car. Two men presided, one cooking and the other waiting on the table. We were laboriously spearing our food with two tined forks, and sipping the muddy coffee with a pewter spoon, when I heard with surprise the general asking for a napkin. It seemed as foreign to the place as a finger-bowl. The waiter knew him, however,

> and liked him too well to refuse him anything; so he said, "I have nothing but a towel, general." "Just the thing, just the thing," repeated my husband, in his quick, jolly way. So the man tied a long crash towel under his chin, and the general ate on, too indifferent to appearances to care because the tableful of travellers smiled.[8]

The flat car eating house at Fargo was not long in service. The railroad's boardinghouse was remodeled when its boarders followed the end of the track westward, and it opened for business as the Headquarters Hotel on April 1, 1873.[9]

On June 3, the rails were laid into a new city on the east bank of the Missouri named Edwinton for Edwin Johnson—but soon to be renamed Bismarck to honor the company's German bondholders. Construction of the largest and most magnificent of hotels yet built on the NP was begun just east of the depot at Bismarck. This was the Sheridan House, christened to memorialize another hero of the late rebellion, Lt. Gen. Philip H. Sheridan, then commander of the Military Division of the Missouri, headquartered at Chicago. Sheridan's command included the Department of the Dakota, where the Sioux barred NP progress beyond the Missouri in 1873. The Indians had agreed in treaties to allow the railroad to cross their unceded territory, but they well understood that white settlers followed the railroad. He had replaced the few detachments of infantry from Fort Rice that had been assigned to protect the engineers with the Seventh Cavalry, based at Fort Lincoln, and the mounted Sioux met mounted enemies. Three years later, the way west was secured.[10]

Yet, it was not Indians who represented a threat to the NP's financial fortunes in 1873. Bond sales had thinned to a trickle and rail freight traffic revenues dwindled as the nation's farmers reacted to falling commodity prices by sharply cutting back on sales of grain and kindred farm

products. And nothing in those days could shake the confidence of America the way a declining farm economy could. All investors, great and small, crawled into their shells. Lacking the income to meet scheduled interest payments, Cooke took momentary refuge behind closed doors. That set off the panic.[11]

The sudden demise of Cooke's bond sales cut off the vital flow of construction funds to the Northern Pacific, which, as a result, went into receivership April 16, 1874. Momentarily, it appeared the charter would be revoked, but Frederick Billings came forth with a plan of reorganization that calmed and satisfied all holders of NP securities, as well as the bankruptcy court, and the company was reborn in 1875 under the aegis of a Billings-led group of NP enthusiasts determined to restore financial integrity and resume construction as quickly as prudent management would permit. From 1873 to 1879, branch roads were built in Washington Territory and Minnesota; the company reached the Twin Cities by building rail line and buying trackage rights; the first of the giant bonanza wheat farms was established in Dakota; and, at long last, work was resumed on the main line west of Bismarck.[12]

The Custers again rode an NP train in March 1876, less than four months before the lieutenant colonel led his troops to disaster at the Little Big Horn. That winter the railroad operated no trains west of Fargo but planned to resume service April 1. Custer, returning from a visit to the East, argued so forcefully in favor of a special train that NP officials relented. Mrs. Custer provided an idealized account of the incident:

> When we reached St. Paul the prospect before us was dismal, as the trains were not to begin running until April, at the soonest. The railroad officials, mindful of what the general had done for them in protecting their advance workers in the building of the road, came and offered to open the route. . . .

> The train on which we finally started was an immense one, and certainly a curiosity. There were two snowploughs and three enormous engines; freight-cars with coal supplies and baggage; several cattle-cars, with stock belonging to the Black Hills miners who filled the passenger-coaches. There was an eating-house, looming up above everything, built on a flat car. In this car the forty employés of the road, who were taken to shovel snow, etc., were fed. There were several day-coaches, with army recruits and a few passengers, and last of all the paymaster's car, which my husband and I occupied. This had a kitchen and a sitting-room. At first everything went smoothly. The cook on our car gave us excellent things to eat.[12]

Subsequently, snow drifts stranded the train 130 miles west of Fargo, and after six days the Custers were rescued by a sleigh.

The new management apparently gave no thought to regular passenger food service until 1880, and then it was for excursion train patrons, not the general public. In fact, during the NP's first ten years as an operating railroad (1870-79) the company had spent as little as possible on passenger equipment; there was little need for it. The company added perhaps 20 first- and second-class cars in 1871 and early 1872; there are no more records of passenger car purchases until 1879, when the directors authorized the purchase of four "regular" passenger cars, two parlor cars, and one sleeping car.[13]

But in 1880, the company stood at the threshold of a period of furious growth that was fueled by gold and silver strikes in Idaho and refueled by the heaviest invasion of foreign immigrants in the history of the Upper Great Plains. During fiscal 1879, the NP totted up a mere $452,000 in gross passenger, express, and mail revenues, but in fiscal 1884, the total reached more than $4.2

million, an increase of nearly tenfold. What now of the crepe-hangers who had ridiculed the project as "a wild scheme to build a railroad from Nowhere, through No-Man's-Land to No Place"?

In the fall of 1880, the NP acquired two parlor cars. First-class passengers on short, daytime trips wanted something better than day coaches but had no wish to take space in sleeping cars. Chair cars would provide more elbow room—and protect wealthy elbows against any rubbing with poor ones. That same year the NP's roster claimed an "observation car," No. 5001—an office car for the chief engineer of the road, not a passenger vehicle as the name implies. Its low cost of $1,108.83 shows that it must have been a product of the Brainerd Shops.[14]

Also shown on the 1880 equipment list were a business car, a pay car (the one used by Custer and his wife in March 1876), an engineer's car, and, mysteriously, a frontier car. The latter is not otherwise described on the list, nor is its use or acquisition alluded to elsewhere. Moreover, its roster life was brief, for it was replaced in 1881 by, of all things, a dining car.

The evidence suggests that the one became the other, at the hands of Brainerd's now-you-see-it-now-you-don't car-switching wizards. Early in 1881, the business car and an unspecified unit were shopped at Brainerd, the former for a complete refurbishing, the latter to be made into a dining car. Andrew P. Farrar, superintendent of machinery at the shops, addressed General Manager Homer E. Sargent at St.

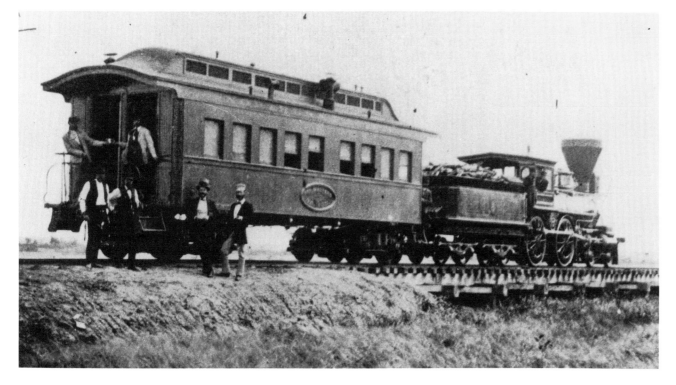

NP paymaster's car, which was used by Gen. George Armstrong and Elizabeth Custer on their last trip to Bismarck, about 1876

Paul on April 8 to ask if the elliptical medallion on the side of the office car should be marked as before, " 'Business Car,' or No. 99 as you spoke of some time ago. . . . We are getting along nicely with the Business Car and [it] is agoing to look splendidly when it is finished." Then he added, "The Dinning [*sic*] Car will be in the Paint shop the latter part of next week [April 10-16]."[15]

The dining car was intended for use in "excursion" trains, unscheduled specials put together for hunters and tourists bent on exploiting the trophy wildlife and uncommon scenery that made the New Northwest a mecca for affluent idlers and bored financiers. Their interest had been piqued by the enticing and amazingly accurate

descriptions of the region that filled the pages of *Harper's Weekly* and other widely circulated periodicals of the day. Among the excursionists was a rising star who would become more adversary than friend, James J. Hill, builder of the Great Northern Railroad. He bought land south of the NP line near Dawson and Steele, Dakota Territory, for a hunting and vacation preserve. Yet he was merely a local phenomenon; countless others who were unknown in the West but who cut a wide swath in the East flocked to capture their share of the excitement generated by easier access to this new promised land. One of these, a bespectacled 25-year-old pilgrim of uncertain health, might very well have been a whiskey drummer for all the interest

OPPOSITE: NP hunting car, 1876
LEFT: NP shops, Brainerd, about 1875

aroused by his passage to Medora, Dakota Territory, in 1883. His name was Theodore Roosevelt, and he was known by cowboy and cattle baron alike as "Old Four Eyes."[16]

Up to 1881, the NP's business cars had been pressed into service for these excursionists' endless wants, but the demand had become so great that the needs of the company were at risk if this practice were to continue. Therefore, the NP's directors decided that additional equipment would be made available for lease to interested parties. Out of this thinking came the railroad's first piece of rolling stock dedicated to the alimentary requirements of its patrons. As Supt. Farrar's crew of artisans put finishing touches on the NP's first dining car, known only as No. 98, Farrar wrote to the general manager on Tuesday, May 24, 1881, presenting a list of china, tableware, and utensils. "If we can get them here by Thursday Morning will have the car ready," he said, as if the road had a china shop, too. But one more thing was needed, he knew: "It will require a first class cook to go with the Dining Car. I do not know

of any man here [Brainerd] that is capable of going with the car. Will you please look up a man in St. Paul[?] He ought to come here at once so as to have it fitted out the way he wants it."[17]

No description of the car is known to have survived, but the superintendent's want list reveals much about it. "Table clothes" were for a 16-foot table. A request for pillows, blankets, and bed linen for only one twin-size bed probably means the waiter would sleep in a room provided or, more likely, on a bunk made by using some of the car's furniture. The china list, including such items as salt cups and egg glasses, napkins and spoon holders, tea cups and saucers, *and* coffee cups and saucers, reveals that this car was far more than a cut above the boarding cars used by the army of workers who were building the road. Excursionists and intimates of officers and directors would henceforth dine in far more splendor than had revenue passengers. But not for long, and the new No. 98 would not survive long enough to become Old 98. For the era of Henry Villard was near at hand.

Henry Villard and the Dining Cars

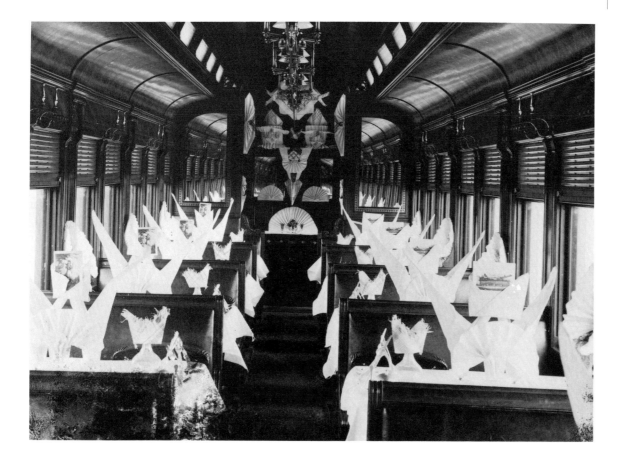

SOON AFTER HIS BIRTH in 1835 at Speyer, in Rhenish Bavaria, Ferdinand Heinrich Gustav Hilgard began to exhibit the independence of spirit and action that would mark him for the rest of his life. As a precocious 13-year-old, he became caught up in Germany's campus unrest of 1848-49. His jurist father, mindful of his own political future, sent him to various schools in order to separate him from the prevailing revolutionary climate; the son finally concluded that his own and his father's political sympathies would never coincide. To spare his parents further embarrassment, he set out for the United States at the age of 18. Concern for his father's political future led him to adopt the name Henry Villard—reminiscent of his given name but actually that of a schoolmate—while still aboard the ship that was taking him to the New World. Penniless, he borrowed $20 from a shipboard acquaintance as the vessel was being nudged into New York harbor.[1]

During the ensuing four years he wrote articles for a German-language newspaper, read law, and taught school, all the while learning to read and write English. His talent for the latter led him to a career as a political reporter.

His success was immediate and satisfying. Editors trusted his talent and mature judgment almost from the outset. He became a free-lance journalist, covering the Minnesota constitutional convention in 1857 for the *New York Tribune*, the Lincoln-Douglas debates in 1858 for the *New York Staats-Zeitung*, the Pike's Peak gold rush in 1859 and the Republican convention of 1860 for the *Cincinnati Commercial*. After the presidential election, Villard was engaged by the *New York Herald* to stay with president-elect Abraham Lincoln, who had become his personal friend, from his election until inauguration day.

When war broke out in 1861 he became a phenomenally successful war correspondent, venturing fearlessly into danger and reporting on the war's major battles. At war's end he married Fanny Garrison, daughter of the arch-abolitionist, William Lloyd Garrison, and then resumed his career as a correspondent in Europe. In 1871 his health deteriorated, and he spent nearly three years in Germany recuperating.

During a prolonged stay in Wiesbaden, he occupied empty hours by dabbling in investments, especially American securities. When the crash of 1873 propelled many U.S. railroads into bankruptcy, German bondholders were prominent among the victims. Leading banks formed protective associations in an effort to minimize losses and, if possible, to salvage something for the future. Bankers in Berlin, Frankfurt, and Heidelberg induced Villard to join several of the committees. Later, they asked him to go to America as their personal representative to negotiate a repayment scheme that both sides could live with.

In 1874 Villard negotiated just such an agreement to reorganize the Oregon and California Railroad Company, which had suffered under shocking mismanagement. The bondholders made him president of the O&C and the Oregon Steamship Company in 1876; deliberately but prudently, he organized for them a series of companies designed to gain control of each mode of transportation that radiated from the mouth of the river, with Portland serving as the control center.

At first, the horizon was free of clouds and as blue as the eyes that scanned it. But as 1880 dawned, he thought he detected something like the birth of a storm cloud to the east. What he saw in his mind's eye was, of course, the dust cloud rising from the Northern Pacific's resumption of construction in Dakota and Montana. The NP's Frederick Billings not only planned to complete the line all the way to the Pacific, he refused Villard's offer to share the use of his Oregon Railroad and Navigation Company's trackage on the Columbia's south bank, choosing instead to run a line along the opposite shore. This was unacceptable, of course—not just for Henry Villard, but for the bondholders who had employed him to protect their interests.

As he cast about for the means to ensure continued success of these enterprises, he came up with a revolutionary concept in the history of corporation management, a concept that soon was much copied and which is in wide use a century later. Villard reasoned that if he could gain ascendancy in the affairs of the Northern Pacific through purchase of a majority of its stock, he could then create a company in which would be invested control of both the NP and his OR&N, while they would continue to be managed separately. The parent company could exert sufficient influence in their board rooms to require cooperation and forestall actions that could lead to destructive competition. Thus would be born what we now call the holding company.[2]

In February 1881, he circulated a confidential memo among some 50 of his American and European investor friends, inviting them to join him in subscribing to an $8 million fund. He would reveal its purpose to them on or before May 15. Such was the confidence they had come to place in his financial sagacity that within 24 hours the fund was oversubscribed; in fact, the desire to participate was so intense that he was offered more than double the amount he had requested. What would become known as "Villard's Blind Pool" was a rousing success. Then, before Billings and his supporters knew what he was about, Villard bought enough NP common stock to become majority shareholder and implement his programs.

Between June 1870 and September 1881, when Villard was elected to the board and then the presidency, the company had built but 990 miles of line. The group in power was content to move ahead cautiously, determined to complete the main line but to hold back enough cash to serve as a buffer against another economic disaster. Villard knew better than those fearfully conservative, status-quo plodders that a "one-gut" railroad was destined to starve in the long run, that survival demanded a strong network of feeder lines to bring in the stuff of which profits were made. In 30 months of fund raising, he secured $40 million in financing and masterminded not only completion of the main line, but construction of 700 miles of branch lines across the system. In all, 1,586 additional

miles of railroad were built and placed in operation during that brief span. Even more important to the NP's existence, and without which there could be no freight to haul, was the means to bring in people, the farmers and merchants and artisans who would settle the land and the tourists who would take the word back east that there was more than desert waste in the West. So he set out to enhance passenger business by altering company philosophy and beefing up the equipment roster.[3]

In July 1879, the Billings board had canceled the NP's Pullman contract and decreed that "all 'sleeping' and . . . 'parlor cars,' regularly run on the lines of road operated by the Company, shall be owned, controlled and managed by it." This pinch-penny policy did not help. "Passenger,

Henry Villard

Express and Mail" revenue for the preceding year had totaled just over $450,000. In the ensuing two years it rose to $636,000 and $783,000, respectively. At the end of that period, the NP owned only seven sleeping cars, two parlor cars and 29 first-, second-, and third-class coaches.[4]

Enter Villard. As an immigrant and a well-traveled journalist, Villard had acquired a broad education in third-class accommodations and he knew what it was to scratch and grabble his way about the country. He seized the opportunity to challenge the status quo. The NP's third-class coaches were upgraded to second class; emigrant sleepers were introduced; a new contract was negotiated with the Pullman Company; the passenger car fleet was expanded; and an internal dialogue on the merits of adding dining cars to cross-country trains was initiated.

The results of his crusade for comfort were startling. Fiscal 1882 income from passenger, mail, and express operations almost doubled that of the previous year, rising to over $1.5 million. In the following year it skyrocketed to more than $2.4 million.[5] To make all this possible, Villard had invested in one man an uncommon degree of authority and then given his passenger department more responsibility than it had ever enjoyed.

Villard's good right hand was Thomas F. Oakes, who possessed extraordinary talent for rail building and operations. The two had met when the latter was general superintendent of the Kansas Pacific Railroad and Villard was a receiver of that company. In 1880 the Boston native accepted Villard's invitation to join him in Portland to become manager of the new Oregon Railway and Navigation Company. Then, after the German gained control of the NP, Oakes was elected both NP board member and first vice president. From this position, as Villard's surrogate, Oakes took virtual command of the NP in the field, while the man who put him there devoted his time to raising money. Both men accomplished their missions. Yet neither ignored the public relations aspects of the undertaking.

Villard and Oakes evidently thought that if investors (especially the European investors Villard knew) and the general public were to be impressed with the Northern Pacific's potential, the company would have to offer the very best passenger service available anywhere in the United States. That is, all travelers must be coddled to the utmost. This meant finding an alternative to those eating places that NP management had suffered to exist in the past. One alternative, of course, was that which all other railroads in the West had seen fit to outlaw, dining cars. Yet neither Villard nor Oakes was of a mind to commit himself to this expense if operating department personnel were prepared to advance sound arguments against it. Accordingly, on November 14, 1882, Oakes put the question to Gen. Herman Haupt, the NP's new general manager and the builder and rebuilder of Lincoln's Civil War railroads in Virginia.[6]

Three days later, Haupt relayed the question to his superintendent of transportation, George W. Cross. The latter was a man whose health wavered woefully under the stresses of his job and who had grown timid in dealings with his superiors. He consulted with his staff before finally making a hesitant reply on November 30. "To equip the Road with Dining Cars would be a very considerable expense. The furniture and fixtures of each car would cost $2500.00;—the wear and tare [*sic*] on which would be 25% greater than is usual in restaurants: the cost of service, i.e., Conductor, Cooks, and waiters would be $320 per month per car; the great length of the Line to transport supplies over would add to the expense and chance of failure at times when it would be seriously felt; and as these cars would be required particularly in the underdeveloped region west of Glendive, I would suggest they could hardly be made profitable, and it might be difficult to make them a good advertisement for the Road."[7]

Cross tentatively recommended that the Northern Pacific build "commodious and attractive Dining halls, with Waiting-rooms and Ticket Offices." These trackside

NP train, about 1885

facilities could be "operated by the Company as a Hotel Dept. under the supervision of Mr. [Ellis J.] Westlake and suitable Assistants," he suggested. In fact, he thought the hotel that recently had been destroyed by fire at Brainerd could now be replaced by such a restaurant as "a good point to experiment on." That there were drawbacks to his plan he was well aware. Cross noted that the hotels at Fargo and Jamestown were "certainly very objectionable to our patrons and the cause of much criticism of the Road." Nevertheless, he felt certain they could be improved and earn a profit. At the same time, he was wary of going *too* far with his criticism. His letter, dictated to and handwritten by his secretary, initially ended on a confident note: "Certainly it is a matter of vital importance to the Road to have the passengers['] meals clean, palatable and wholesome, which they are not now on our Line"—to which Cross cautiously added in his own hand the qualifier, "as a rule," before signing.

But his letter was all for naught. Fainthearted George Cross simply had taken too much time to formulate his cautiously critical response. Villard and Oakes already had decided in favor of dining cars, and the contract with Pullman's Palace Car Company for 10 dining cars was executed on November 22, 1882, eight days before Cross mailed his letter to the general manager. Four months later, his name disappeared from the NP's list of officers, having been replaced by that of the former superintendent of the Dakota Division, Jabez T. Odell, who was known throughout the railroad as a formidable taskmaster.[8]

Villard was personally involved in planning for NP passenger equipment, making the final decisions on types of cars and their accoutrements in virtually every instance. For example, in a letter to George Pullman dated November 3, 1882, Oakes confirmed a verbal order for 50 first-class passenger coaches and noted, "I find in talking over with Mr. Villard the matter of the construction of these cars that he is strongly of the opinion in view of the long runs to be made that at least one-half of the coaches

should have head and shoulder rests for the passengers." Oakes thought that these requirements could be met "without disfiguring the interior of the car."

The five weeks between November 3 and December 18 must have been an especially busy period for the two decision makers. In that time orders for the 50 first-class coaches, 20 second-class coaches, and 17 emigrant sleepers, as well as for the 10 dining cars, were placed with Pullman, who agreed to a delivery schedule he should have known he could not meet. Villard had set his sights on mid-1883 as a general target date for completion of the main stem, however, and already he was making plans for an unprecedented celebration of the event, the centerpiece for which would be his fine new passenger trains. As it turned out, both goals eluded the grasp of the men who had set them. But the stage was set for a publicity barrage.

Pullman himself used the car orders to promote his operations in newspapers and magazines, in particular, those of the Chicago area. A long article appearing in the Chicago *Inter-Ocean* for December 20, just two days after the fourth contract had been signed, included the announcement: "The [Pullman] Company is now commencing work on ten dining cars for the Northern Pacific Railroad, which are to be ready in June. . . . An order has been obtained from the Northern Pacific for sixty passenger coaches and thirty-seven second class cars, which are to be delivered as soon as possible."[9] This article was pirated by almost all the railroad-oriented publications in the country in the next two months.

For the time, at least, Oakes and other NP officers were content to let Pullman tell the story. They devoted their time to choosing new paint schemes for passenger cars and new uniforms for conductors and trainmen, deciding on the number and diameter of wheels, and so forth. George W. Cushing, superintendent of motive power, machinery, and rolling stock, spent three days at the Pullman Works in Chicago to ensure that all of Villard's and Oakes's expectations would be realized. While repeating the understanding that "All effort at extra display [is] to be avoided," his detailed report to Oakes also indicated standards for the dining cars: "All finish to be of best character, and fittings and furnishings to be first class of their kind and such as good taste and judgment would expect to find in a Northern Pacific Dining Car. The side board is to be of elegant design and perfectly adapted to the use intended. This will also supply the lunch feature so far as it is practicable in the car."[10]

Although Villard might be expected to seek an experienced hand to head up the new department for dining car service, he clearly felt pressed for time and was probably convinced that the field was far too new to have produced true veterans. Whatever the reason, Villard's choice was the man who had supervised the NP's hotels and restaurants for several years. Circular No. 55 was issued from St. Paul on March 5, 1883:

> *E. J. Westlake has been appointed Superintendent of Dining Cars on Northern Pacific Railroad, to take effect April 1st, proximo.*
>
> *The supervision of this office will also extend to Hotels and Restaurants along the line of the N. P. R. R. so far as to examine and report whether conditions of leases are complied with in reference to the character of meals and accommodations furnished to travelers and employees.*[11]

This appointment should have been made earlier, but the NP's tardiness was anything but reprehensible. Perhaps management was aware of Pullman's reputation for late deliveries and artful manipulation of invoices. A good illustration of both may be seen in its handling of the order for those 50 first-class coaches.

By terms of the contract, these cars should have been received between March 1 and July 31, 1883. On April 7 Pullman wrote Oakes that "Mr. Villard went with me through the works at Pullman and saw quite a number of the cars which we are building for your company." It is easy to imagine that Pullman kept up a running dialogue about money and delivery dates, promising much, yielding little, and asking for a great deal. He reminded Oakes that 34 cars would be shipped to the NP during the month, noting, with no apology, that Pullman would be "obliged to put in ten West Shore 2nd class cars, the construction of which is identical with your own." These, he assured Oakes, could be used by the NP until it received "a sufficient number of first class cars." Shamelessly—not a car had been delivered yet—he asked for partial payment "on account, for our accommodation," reporting that Villard was entirely agreeable to such an arrangement.[12]

In fact, only 11 cars of NP ownership were shipped that month, and the initial delivery of five first-class coaches was made July 28, nearly nine months after 50 had been ordered. The last were exposed to daylight on September 21, well after the NP needed them for its first through trains. In addition, some two and one-half months after the order had been placed, Pullman's contracting agent, L. G. Matthews, had asked the NP to buy and furnish the wheels specified for the cars. As a result, the railroad ordered the parts from the Allen Paper Car Wheel Company and paid for them separately.[13]

When the first 10 coaches were delivered, the NP discovered that they failed to conform to specifications. Consequently, and with Pullman's acquiescence, they were used with the understanding that the railroad could exchange them later. Pullman had agreed to replace them with 13 emigrant sleepers, the cost for which would have been $1,758.13 less than that for the 10 coaches. Yet, when Pullman submitted a bill for final settlement of all accounts, it included charges for the 10 coaches, the 13 emigrant sleepers, *and* the cost of wheels plus a 10 percent commission on them! By that time, the NP had already paid for the coaches, had returned them, and had not received the sleepers.

Fortunately, the company's James B. Williams, assistant to the president, was a match for George Pullman's creative accountants. "The last page of Bill of items," he wrote, "might as well have been put down [as] Sundries for all the information it contains." He balked at the charge for profit on wheels, as well as that for equipment that Pullman had asked to furnish at cost. He refused to pay a $2.40 switching charge against each of the 10 cars; after all, the NP had taken delivery in Chicago and had been billed by the railroad involved. No payment was made until the car builder's people had corrected the billing.

The NP fared somewhat better with its diners. Pullman ran the first dining car, No. 201, out of the shops on April 16 and hauled it to Chicago's Union Station. The following day, the Northern Pacific showed him how to stage a public relations event. The *Inter-Ocean* gave a full account:

A NEW DINING CAR

The first of a number of new dining cars to be run on the Northern Pacific Road was shown to a company of railroad and journalistic gentlemen yesterday afternoon at the Union Depot [Station]. There are ten of these cars which are to be run from St. Paul to points along the line. They are sixty-six feet in length and are finished in mahogany and natural woods, the ceiling being of light hardwood, ornamented with hand-painted flowers. There are ten tables and forty seats, which can be turned up when not in use. A novel feature is the sideboard at one end of the car, while another is the funnel in the kitchen over the range, which absorbs the heat and odors of the car.

A fine lunch was served and at its conclusion the following was unanimously adopted:

"The Northern Pacific Railway [sic] Company, in inaugurating a line of dining-cars for its vast system, soon to be completed from Lake Superior to the Pacific Ocean, has shown an enterprise and care for the

comfort of the many thousands who are soon to travel over its lines which commands the strongest recommendation. The new car which we have had the pleasure, under the courteous supervision of Mr. A[lfred] L. STOKES, Assistant Superintendent of Traffic of the Oregon Railroad and Navigation and Northern Pacific Companies, of examining, is one of the finest specimens of the Pullman Company's artistic and durable work. It is difficult to see how comfort and luxury could be more perfectly combined than in this car, which is one of half a score to fly across the plains of Dakota and the mountains of Idaho and Montana, carrying delighted tourists over this new highway across the continent. That this company has already placed upon its new line such a magnificent system of sleeping and dining cars is an evidence that it does not intend to be in any respect behind any of the older railways of the country."[14]

The reporter for *Railway Age* (Chicago) took a more jocular approach to the episode, but closed on a note that betrayed both astonishment and a need to dissemble lest he appear too naïve for a big-city magazine writer:

The Northern Pacific railroad company is about to literally "astonish the natives" of Minnesota, Dakota, Montana, Idaho, Washington territory and Oregon— including Indians, buffaloes, bears and other early settlers—by placing upon its long route over the continent a line of dining cars of the most luxurious character, really first class hotel tables on wheels. The first of these cars was exhibited a day or two ago in this city to a select company of railway men and newspaper representatives, Mr. A. L. Stokes, of the Northern Pacific and Oregon Railway and Navigation companies, being the host, assisted by Mr. E. J. Westlake, superintendent of the dining car line. When it is stated that the Pullman company had carte

blanche to build as fine a car as possible, and that the silverware alone cost a thousand dollars, superlatives in regard to the construction and equipment of the car are unnecessary.[15]

No. 201 was deadheaded west in a Chicago and Northwestern train, arriving in St. Paul on April 20. Two more diners, Nos. 204 and 207, joined it on April 23 and 27. They were pressed into service for training the new crews, but only briefly, then put on trains to operate between St. Paul and Fargo about May 1, 1883.

Two switchmen, one at Fargo, the other in St. Paul, soon had reason to regret the company's reaching a new milestone in passenger service.

At Fargo, switchman Charles Jones, contrary to yard rules, had cut off No. 207 from train No. 1, the westbound *Pacific Express*, and rode it onto another track where No. 2, the eastbound *Atlantic Express,* was about to depart for Moorhead. He failed to apply the brakes and rammed into the rear of the standing train with such force that everything was thrown off the tables. Among the articles broken were 18 crystal water goblets and nine wine glasses. Although the total value of the loss was set at an almost undiscernible $6.38, Jones was summarily discharged for "poor Judgement and Carelessness." The verdict was identical in St. Paul for an unnamed switchman who, on May 7, had the misfortune of riding No. 201 into the rear of a train at the St. Paul Union Depot. In this collision, even the shelves were swept clean of china, crystal, condiments, and silver. When the contents of the wine cellar flew to the floor, a bottle of champagne and three bottles of wine drenched the carpet. The value of the broken items in this instance was four times greater than in the Fargo accident. Fortunately, No. 204 was standing by and could be run in as a replacement. Superintendent of Transportation Odell fired off a letter to all division superintendents that put every train employee on notice "in reference to the careful handling of these cars."[16]

Meanwhile, Pullman was making plans to use the newest of the NP dining cars as one of his entries for the Railway Appliance Exposition scheduled to open May 24 in Chicago, the city that Carl Sandburg would memorialize three decades later as "Player with Railroads." Just about the time a westbound *Pacific Express* left St. Paul with the first dining car ever used in regular service by the Northern Pacific, Pullman workers were trundling the newly completed dining car No. 206 through the high doors of their plant and out onto the house track. Of course, No. 206 was probably subjected to closer inspections and no doubt caused more elbow strain than any of its siblings. It was to be a rolling advertisement for Pullman's wares, especially his dining cars, which were now recipients of most of his personal affections and the creation in which were invested his fondest hopes for greater future success.

Like most shows of its kind, Chicago's huge exposition was more than a sideshow for tourists and would-be travelers in the host city; it was a place for builders to sell and for builders and prospective buyers to gauge public reaction to the equipment on the floor. In addition, it offered car builders an opportunity to prove the advertised superiority of their wares over those of their most zealous competitors. Gold medals would be awarded to the best in show in each class of equipment. Pullman had pioneered such cars, and he meant to maintain his lead over newcomers in the field. The Northern Pacific might have to wait for this particular car—but the railroad would share in the good publicity, and the entire order was being completed ahead of schedule.

Despite the foot-dragging that accompanied work on the road's first-class coaches and other cars, it was obvious that all of the diners would be shipped before the date for final delivery was reached. Although news reports in December 1882 carried the announcement that they would be completed in June, the contract was somewhat more liberal in its demands. Oakes had asked for six of them "as soon as practicable," then one each month between June and September. According to George Cushing's files, cars 206 and 209, the last of the lot, were received July 13, 1883. Evidently, it suited the millionaire's purpose to get his showcase on the road as soon as possible, to paraphrase Oakes's request.[17]

Meanwhile, the month-long railroad spectacle generated extensive coverage by the world's press and wire services. Pullman could not buy better, more effective advertising. The *Railway Review* (Chicago) of June 16, 1883, offered a detailed account of the exhibits under the dry heading, "The Exposition." After a brief description of the trade fair's parameters, it noted:

> *Dining Car No. 206 for the Northern Pacific is from the Pullman shops. This is a very long car, being some 76 feet from out to out of drawheads, affording a large and commodious kitchen. There is a double passage from the dining room around the sideboard to the serving room, so that the waiters do not have to meet each other while passing to and fro. This car has a dark outside finish, as is the balance of the Northern Pacific passenger equipment, and is furnished with 6-wheeled trucks and Allen 42-inch wheels.*[18]

Twelve days later, the *Inter-Ocean* carried a list of the show's top prize winners. Under "Class No. 2-cars" was revealed, "Best dining, gold medal, Pullman Palace Car Company." This was the hope realized—but the show's benefits carried on. A month later the *Railroad Gazette* (New York) mentioned the display and betrayed its attitude toward the car's staff: "The Pullman Palace Car Company exhibited a day coach for the New York, West Shore & Buffalo Railroad, also a dining car for the Northern Pacific lines, with all the furniture, china-ware, etc., including a porter."[19]

The "dark outside finish" mentioned in the *Railway Review* was another Villard-Oakes effort to spruce up the

NP's image. Yellow in an infinite variety of tonal shadings had been the color of preference among pioneer railroads and car builders for nearly half a century. A mature line needed something that hinted of majesty and financial stability. Paint schemes became the subject of widespread internal discussion almost from the moment the two executives came onto the property.

Two weeks before Villard's election to the presidency, Oakes obtained "one set of ornamental coach patterns" and paint samples from Haupt, who had requested them from A. P. Farrar, superintendent of machinery at Brainerd. Farrar reported that the bright, yellowish white used on NP passenger equipment was arrived at by mixing "22-1/2# White Lead in oil [with] 15# Golden Ochre in oil." Lettering, corners, doors, medallions, and belt rail were painted Tuscan Red, while the trucks and platforms were finished in Brandon Yellow. It was a theme worthy of a P. T. Barnum circus train.[20]

In January 1882, George Cross was asked for his opinion on colors for the new passenger equipment. He promptly recommended that "these cars be painted dark red, the same color and paint as used by the Penna R.R. Co."—a wine or burgundy red. He said that company had experimented "extensively and expensively" with various schemes but had found Pennsy Red to be more serviceable and less expensive than "the yellow or any other color."[21]

This open forum on color continued almost to the day a decision had to be made. And in the end, Villard and Oakes agreed it would be best to go along with Pullman's own dark green on all cars. In a letter to Haupt on November 27, 1882, Cushing reminded him of the change: "As you are aware the color of coaches has been changed to the Pullman color."[22] For the next nine decades, the Northern Pacific passenger equipment would sport green livery in any number of combinations, even after it became part of the new Burlington Northern. However, car interiors were changed radically with each new order, although none ever surpassed the Villard-era decor for

sheer artistry, craftsmanship, and elegance. Whatever one thought of George Pullman at that time, none could deny his way with car interiors.

The former cabinetmaker brought to his life's work an affinity for wood that few other car builders could match. In the NP's dining cars, for example, he incorporated materials derived from no fewer than 14 different species of tree, native and alien—"mahogany and natural woods," as the *Inter-Ocean* reporter put it.[23] Mahogany was far from the rarest of woods used, although it was the most expensive, having been brought from Africa and the West Indies. Primavera was a yellowish-white stock from Central America that is far more current among furniture makers today. Basswood, the American linden tree, was used freely in NP diners; as a strong yet "soft" hardwood, it is now much prized by woodcarvers and sculptors. Tulipwood and poplar, as well as basswood, are used now only in inexpensive, mass-produced furniture items. To Pullman they all were as commonplace as money.

He apparently felt that his knowledge of the finer things extended to china, crystal, and silver, too. On January 26, 1883, he wrote to Oakes about the dining car furnishings, accessories, and equipment with the object of forestalling any moves by the railroad to intrude into an area where he believed he excelled:

> [I] beg to suggest that the quality and design of the table furniture and linen should be in harmony with the general character and design of the cars; and I think that greater economy and more satisfactory results could be obtained by allowing us to furnish the cars complete. . . .

> We will, however, with great pleasure arrange this matter as you may decide, after receiving this letter.[24]

Oakes gave in to the whim, but that decision would be the cause of much concern to James B. Williams as he dealt with the bill a year later. Pullman ensured that the cars were supplied with everything conductors, cooks, waiters, or patrons ever would have need for, including a monkey wrench, a screw driver, a gimlet, and four spittoons. Williams would question the use of spittoons in dining cars, but he showed quiet concern when confronted by Pullman's audacity in billing the NP repeatedly for 10 percent profit on materials he had requested to furnish at cost. Of course, everything was of the best quality, and the NP would truly have no need to take a backseat to any other line. Supt. Cushing may well have summed it up best when he crowed in his January 23, 1883, letter to Oakes, "I think these cars will be everyway satisfactory to the travel, and quite as good as those the Union Pacific will be able to furnish, although they may make more show."[25]

The Union Pacific, of course, was by now well aware of what the NP was doing, but the acknowledged leader of the western lines was yet inclined, no doubt, to let the northern upstart learn the hard way that there would be no profits from such extravagance. They might well have paid more attention to Villard and what he was up to. But even if they had watched him closely, it is doubtful they could have guessed the reasons behind his actions. A railroad celebration of the scope he was planning had never been imagined before, much less pulled off. The Northern Pacific's dining cars could be said to be central to that celebration. Well, if not central, at least crucial.

OPPOSITE: The interior of a dining car built in 1900 reflected a continued commitment to elegant decor.

Across the Continent

EFORE 1883, FEW EVENTS HAD BEEN considered important enough to bring together heads of state or their high-ranking personal emissaries. And certainly no one but a Henry Villard would ever dream that a used and rusty iron spike being driven into a rude wooden tie in a remote mountain valley in the largely uninhabited American West could accomplish that very thing. But dream it he did, and to the amazement of many, he succeeded.[1]

A cynic might suggest that Villard wanted dining cars *only* because he needed them for his grand celebration. After all, he could not expect nobility, government representatives, and prominent dignitaries to sit ignominiously on NP lunch-counter stools.   On the other hand, the equipment was needed to provide the NP's patrons with every comfort they had a right to expect. The evidence clearly shows his commitment to the service over the long haul.

Soon after he gained control of NP management in 1881, Villard made several key decisions aimed at upgrading and expanding both freight and passenger service. Oakes was sent out immediately to examine the lands lying between the ends of track, to gauge their productivity, and to make traffic projections. After describing the region (essentially the entire territory of Montana) he estimated that the gross earnings of the Northern Pacific for 1882-83 would be $6.1 million—more than double the road's revenues in fiscal 1881 and $1.8 million short of the actual total. Villard might well have believed the projection to be conservative, because his orders in that two-year period more than tripled NP freight car ownership and nearly quadrupled its passenger train fleet. Freight and miscellaneous earnings for fiscal 1883 were two and one-half times the total for fiscal 1881, and income from passenger train operations more than tripled it. As for the dining cars, which made no significant contribution to income until fiscal 1884, Villard's actions make his motives clear. As soon as the ninth and tenth units of the initial purchase were delivered, he personally ordered four more—not to use in his last-spike excursion trains, but to ensure that the company had a sufficient number to equip all the trains he expected to have operating on long main- and branch-line runs before year's end.

In mid-July, too, planning for the grand event was complete and invitations sent. The meeting of steel from east and west was expected to take place during the first week of September, so Villard chose Saturday, September 8, as the day for concluding ceremonies at a site in Montana's Deer Lodge Valley. Obviously, he was relieved when the track ends were joined at 3:00 P.M. on Wednesday, August 22.

The show went on as planned. It was a celebration that defied adjectives. The railroad's publicist noted that it had been described as an excursion, "a word that was altogether inadequate"; he preferred to regard it as "an expedition." And so it was. Three hundred sixty-two guests accepted invitations to see the deed accomplished. There were official agents of six northern European governments, not to mention 66 German and British guests representing commercial, scientific, industrial, parliamentary, military, and journalistic interests. From the U.S. there were a dozen governors and former governors, members of the legislative, executive, and judicial branches of the federal government, and 39 publishers and journalists, including such luminaries as Joseph Pulitzer and Carl Schurz. And the trains that hauled this army of celebrants were made up of the very cream of private cars borrowed from eastern roads, plus Villard's newly acquired cars for the transcontinental passenger service that would begin daily following the party. There were five trains in all, one from the West Coast, using the best equipment the OR&N had to offer, and four from St. Paul, two of which included the new dining cars from the Pullman works. They were greeted and feted by townspeople at all the major stops on the way.

The mixed army of journalists, foreign and domestic, whom Villard had invited gave proper publicity to the festivities. Representatives of the large-circulation

newspapers and magazines in the East and in Europe produced myriad accounts that covered every possible aspect of the drama—the land, the settlers, the players, the scenery, and the props—except the dining cars. Many Montana reporters came to observe the festivities, but since none had ridden the trains, their comments on the subject were limited to brief mentions in their descriptions of the trains and complaints about the absence of food for spectators.

An exception was Nicolaus Mohr, a German publisher from Bremen. He kept a diary during his long journey and from time to time sent excerpts back home to his paper. His entry for September 10 told of crossing the Snake River in Washington Territory on a ferry:

> Transporting the whole train took an endlessly long time, so long that one of my press colleagues picked up his gun and went out hunting. But it looked to me as though he used his gun less skillfully than his pen. Our cook gave him instructions, but he still had no success.
>
> The cook, incidentally, is also a German. He came from Frankfurt to America with his father who is now the owner of a well-established confectionery in New York. . . . If I am not mistaken, he was hired specially for this Northern Pacific trip at a salary of four-hundred dollars.

On the return trip, some eight days later, Mohr provided his readers with a description of the food service on the new diners:

> At first we were overcome by a feeling of imprison-ment as we settled down once more in our Pullman Sleeping Car. But then we do have access to the dining car, which also serves as kitchen and store-room.
>
> By German standards, our accommodations are luxurious. We follow the American pattern of eating.

> This means meat, fish, and eggs with morning coffee or tea; light lunch at one o'clock; and dinner not until seven o'clock in the evening. Every day we get fresh, hot bread. But although the Americans mean well, we who care about our stomachs truly would prefer what they call "stale bread." Our car has a very good wine cellar, with Bordeaux, Rhine wine, Moselle, and Champagne. Then too Milwaukee beer and mineral water are available.[2]

Another writer was Eugene V. Smalley, whom Villard had hired away from the *New York Tribune* to publicize the NP and its territory. Smalley did not neglect the opportunity to promote the luxurious accommodations in his magazine, *The Northwest*:

> In the dining-cars the meals were bountiful in quantity and excellent in quality. Ducks from the Dakota ponds, trout from the Yellowstone [River], venison from the Rocky Mountains, and salmon from the Columbia, were added to the regular bills of fare in the course of the trip. There was nothing to indicate the great distance from markets and cities, save the occasional necessity of resorting to condensed milk for the coffee.[3]

Smalley's new magazine had carried advertising for the diners since April, when a full-page NP display ad heralded their arrival. The list of the line's attractions ended with: "The finest Dining Cars in the land, in which first-class meals will be served en route at 75 cents."[4]

Through the rest of that year, the advertisement's main copy varied from one issue to the next, but the last line remained the same. In August, as the cars were readied for operation, the words "will be served" were changed to "are served" and the service was specified for "all through trains." (Beginning that month, too, the ad carried a bold headline, produced by an apparently prescient copywriter, who anointed the NP as "THE GREAT NORTHERN

TRANSCONTINENTAL ROUTE." Six years later, the essence of this phrase would be adopted as its eponym by another St. Paul-based railroad.)

Late in July, General Passenger and Ticket Agent George P. Barnes introduced a pink pamphlet he entitled *Through Rates of Fare,* quoting fares from St. Paul, Minneapolis, and Duluth through to North Pacific Coast cities and describing the cars of the transcontinental trains. The back cover was devoted to dining car service. Underneath a detailed engraving of an interior view of the car at the dinner hour was printed six lines of doggerel that must have been written to the tempo of a flat-wheeled, third-class coach:

> *To eat when you feel like it and get what you want,*
> *Is the traveler's enjoyment when taking a jaunt:*
> *Therefore, Tourists and others, who are*
>   *on the look out*
> *For solid comfort in travelling and a*
>   *picturesque route,*
> *Take the NORTHERN PACIFIC and in*
>   *dining cars fine,*
> *Enjoy the YELLOWSTONE ROUTE and*
>   *MONTANA SHORT LINE.*

In June, as the NP prepared to put the dining cars in service, John Muir, general superintendent of traffic, told a reporter the projected dates for the inauguration of regular freight and passenger service. "We expect to run through passenger trains between this coast and St. Paul by September 1. . . . The inaugural ceremonies will doubtless take place during the last week in August. . . . The dining-cars, which are becoming so popular in the East, will also be added to the trains at proper places."[5]

Muir's statement set the time closer than any previous announcement. The Villard party lingered in Portland on September 12 when daily transcontinental passenger service between St. Paul and Tacoma, via Portland, was inaugurated under the Northern Pacific flag. Happily, dining car patrons on that first run, and on all that followed, would enjoy the same choice cuisine and friendly service as that provided for Herr Mohr and his fellow world travelers.

In his advertising, Barnes promised diners they could sit down to "a bountiful 'spread' comprising all the DELICACIES OF THE SEASON" from both seaboards, "as well as fish and game obtained from the country through which the road passes." He was as good as his word. For example, the lavish menu prepared for Christmas 1883 offered blue-point oysters, capon with oyster sauce, broiled whitefish, roast beef au jus, roast turkey, stuffed goose, and suckling pig, as well as game that many Dakota and Montana settlers relied on for their daily rations. There were cutlets of quail, fillets of hare, prairie chicken, and saddle of venison. Diversions featured green turtle soup, smoked jowl, pâté de fois gras, Roquefort and Edam cheeses, and garden vegetables in profusion, including "French flageolets," a midget green kidney bean that was rare on any American menu west of New England and little known outside France. And when cutbacks became the order of the day across the NP's system, dining car patrons were not deprived to any degree. The ax fell elsewhere.[6]

None of Villard's guests, apparently, and few but close associates within NP ranks, knew of the financial crisis that faced him and his companies as he approached the day of his triumph. Actually, as early as June he had discovered that all was far from well in the treasury and construction departments. Adna Anderson, the road's chief engineer, had continually assured him that the work would be completed well within budget. But when Anderson filed his year-end report for fiscal 1883, he made the "startling admission" that the costs of finishing the road would exceed the estimates by more than $14 million.[7]

From what he had learned during his recent trip over the line, Villard may have been prepared to hear that the projections would be outstripped, but not by so much as to

93

THE NORTHERN PACIFIC
IS THE
Longest Railway Line
IN THE WORLD
UNDER ONE MANAGEMENT.

NO CHANGE { OF CARS. / OF GAUGE.

All Passenger Trains are Equipped with the Westinghouse Air Brake, Miller Platforms and the Patent Compressed Paper Car Wheels.

Its Track is all Steel Rail, its Road-bed Solid, which permits the greatest speed with perfect safety.

IMPORTANT FACTS
IN REGARD TO THE
NORTHERN PACIFIC RAILROAD.

It is the ONLY "Standard" Gauge Railroad running into Montana Territory.

It is the ONLY Railroad running to Helena, Montana.

It is the ONLY Railroad spanning the entire Territory of Montana.

It is the ONLY Railroad by which passengers can reach Washington Territory, Oregon, Puget Sound Points and British Columbia.

It is the ONLY Trans-Continental Line running Dining cars of any description.

It is the ONLY Railroad running Pullman Sleepers and Elegant Day Coaches through from the East to Montana, Idaho and the Pacific Northwest.

It is the ONLY Railroad running Emigrant Sleepers into Montana, Idaho, Washington and Oregon.

It is the ONLY Rail Route to the Yellowstone National Park; over 100 miles of staging being required by any other route.

HORTON RECLINING CHAIR CARS
ARE RUN BETWEEN
DULUTH AND BRAINERD,
For the Use of First-Class Travel,
FREE OF CHARGE.

wipe out the $13 million in securities that he had reserved as a cushion against unforeseen expenditures. Yet his response to the seeming catastrophe was to console himself and his colleagues with the prospect of greatly accelerated earnings when freight and passengers could be transported across "a through transcontinental line [rather than] one operated in disconnected sections." In fact, he was sure the last spike would signal the end of all his financial worries, as well as the end of construction. He was wrong, and within a few months he had exhausted his personal resources in an effort to stave off the company's creditors. He resigned from the board and the presidency on January 4, 1884.

When the dust from the NP's financial convulsions had settled, new names appeared on many doors, and faces known and nameless had disappeared. General Manager Herman Haupt had abruptly resigned late in October 1883. No reason was given in the bare-bones announcement, which ended with a report that Vice President Oakes would temporarily add the duties of that office to those of his own.[8] Meanwhile, at the other end of the employment ladder, losses were almost beyond counting. The jobs of some 20,000 Chinese, Irish, and Scandinavian tracklayers had come to a more or less natural end with the ritual driving of the last spike. That was to be expected. Not so natural, even if understandable, were the hundreds of job reductions in the ranks of office and mechanical workers.

In the traffic department, there were no layoffs, only a few hirings and a shuffling of the face cards. General Passenger and Ticket Agent G. K. Barnes was shorn of most of his title and made general ticket agent in October 1883, and the name of Charles S. Fee, erstwhile assistant superintendent of traffic, began appearing in NP ads, circulars, and publications as general passenger agent—GPA.

By 1891, when Superintendent of Dining Cars Westlake left the NP, Vice President Oakes had moved responsibility for the dining cars from the general manager to the

GPA. In turn, Fee devoted most of his energies to promoting NP passenger travel business and passed control of day-to-day operations in that department to assistants. However, it soon became obvious that a single supervisor was needed there for continuity of purpose and direction. Therefore, Fee elevated Frank J. Tourtelot to the post vacated by Westlake, his former boss.

Tourtelot inherited a much-praised entity. Although he was no innovator, he made sure there was no deterioration in the quality of food and service offered during his long reign, which did not end until his death in 1908. In 1890, soon after his rise to power, he was challenged by the need to nearly double the work force. The NP had added a second transcontinental train on June 15 that year. As a consequence, the dining car fleet would have to be expanded, so 11 more were acquired, this time from Barney & Smith, of Dayton, Ohio. This order increased the dining car fleet from 13 to 24.[9]

Fee was evidently doing his job very well, indeed. Revenues tripled between 1883 and 1891, from $2.1 million to $6.4 million. Even more startling was the increase in passengers. Some 451,000 rode the company's trains during fiscal 1883. The total fairly leaped to six and one-half times that number in 1890-91. In those eight years, revenue per passenger mile declined from 3.4 cents to 2.6 cents.[10]

Also heartening to Fee and his superiors was the news that the NP continued to dominate the market among travelers to and from the Pacific Northwest in 1891, 18 months after the Union Pacific had installed dining cars on its trains to compete more effectively for that patronage (see table).

The NP's dining car service shared in this growth of patronage, of course. However, its chief consolation was a slight drop in the usual deficit. For example, in fiscal 1886 receipts totaled nearly $134,000. Operating expenses came to about $155,000 and the cost of car maintenance and repairs was more than $16,000. Thus, the loss exceeded

PERCENTAGE OF TRANSCONTINENTAL PASSENGERS CARRIED, 1891

	Westbound	Eastbound
Northern Pacific	45.16	39.46
Canadian Pacific	33.25	28.95
Union Pacific	18.46	18.83
Southern Pacific	2.43	12.76

Source: NP, Annual Report, 1891, p. 22.

$37,000. Eight years later, there was a loss of $28,000 on gross receipts of $317,000. The biggest factor in all the losses was the NP's policy of permitting employees to use the diner at greatly reduced rates. A brakeman would be likely to order the best meal on the menu, when he was asked to pay only 25 cents to partake of food that would cost a revenue passenger from 75 cents to a dollar or more. According to Tourtelot, 41,723 meals were served to employees in 1886. By his reckoning, this contributed nearly $22,000 to that year's deficit.

Losses such as these were the very reason why the CB&Q, the UP, and other western lines declined to offer the service. That the losses were acceptable to the NP is a measure of how well Villard had succeeded in establishing the philosophy that dining cars were as much a part of passenger travel as coaches and sleepers, and that the excess of expenses over revenues was as much a part of the cost of doing business as the cost of locomotive fuel and sand. The period covered by all these statistics was one characterized by unbridled optimism among NP officials and uninhibited expansion of the physical plant. Fueling the fires of their ardor was an income explosion. Revenues for fiscal 1883 were $7.9 million. In eight years they soared to $25.2 million.

Convinced the company was riding upward on a perpetual spiral, the NP's bosses pushed construction and acquisitions without restraint. Trackage operated increased from 1,500 miles in mid-1883 to more than 4,400 by June 30, 1891. Additions to the locomotive fleet lifted units operated, both owned and leased, from 289 to 644, freight cars from 7,500 to 18,500, and passenger train cars from 174 to 370, all in the same span of time. Hotels and lunchrooms were built and purchased from Mandan, North Dakota, to Tacoma. The Wisconsin Central Railroad had been leased to provide the company direct access to Chicago. On the other hand, and as a result of these activities, funded debt had skyrocketed from $39.5 million to an unheard of $125 million.

Even so, generally speaking, the thing most feared among NP officers and board members was the intrusion of unsympathetic competition. The virtually unlimited productive capacity of the territory's agricultural, forest, and mineral lands almost certainly would lure other railroads to seek a share of the bounty. Therefore, if the NP simply uncoiled steel tentacles into the hearts of the richest parts, it could capture forever the lion's share. Unfortunately, the company's managers failed to consider the potentially disastrous effects of a national recession. It must have seemed to them inconceivable that the country could not keep pace with their dreams. But when this eventuality materialized in 1893, they acted with dispatch to minimize their losses and those of the company's investor-owners.

On August 15, 1893, the Northern Pacific Railroad Company went into receivership for the second time in 20 years. When it emerged on July 16, 1896, it was as the Northern Pacific Rail*way*, and its future was assured by the presence, as head of its voting trust, of that incomparable money manager, J. P. Morgan, whose association with the enterprise had begun at the invitation of Henry Villard some 15 years earlier. His assumption of responsibility for the NP's debts was tantamount to guaranteeing its solvency forevermore. Never again was the company afflicted by failure of such magnitude.

Hazen Titus and the Great Big Baked Potato

OVERLEAF: The Great Big Baked Potato, a dining car specialty for more than 60 years. After World War II, the minimum weight dropped from two pounds to one and a half pounds.

WHEN J. P. MORGAN BECAME SAVIOR to the NP, James J. Hill also came to have a voice in its affairs. Hill's role was far smaller than historians and his lionizing biographers have given the world to believe, but somewhat larger than his detractors claim. In scale, it was rather more like a Hollywood superstar's making a cameo appearance in a big-budget movie than that same star's playing the leading role, whatever may be displayed on the marquee.

With the help of British and Canadian financiers, Hill had built the Great Northern Railroad across the continent north of the NP, completing the line in 1893. Later that year, when the NP went into receivership, Hill sought to gain control of it as the first step in his initial bid to arrange a marriage between it and his first love, the GN. This attempt was derailed by the State of Minnesota in 1895. Following the NP's 1896 reorganization, Hill and a number of his friends, including some who were GN stockholders, moved individually to acquire NP stock and were able to buy a bit less than $26 million worth. By May 1, 1901, they had reduced their holdings through sales to about $20 million, Hill himself holding shares worth $7.5 million. The NP's capital structure consisted of common stock worth $80 million and preferred stock valued at $75 million. Thus, while Hill and his GN friends owned substantial amounts of NP stock, it was never enough to give them control.

Hill, with Morgan's acquiescence and financial support, made an ambitious attempt to gain absolute control over rail transportation in the Northwest: he formed the ill-fated Northern Securities holding company late in 1901, six months after the two Northerns had acquired equal and controlling interest in the Chicago, Burlington & Quincy Railroad. Chief opponent to Hill's machinations was E. H. Harriman of the Union Pacific and Southern Pacific, who had sought to purchase the Burlington earlier. When that failed, he tried to take control of the NP and very nearly succeeded when Hill ran out of money to fend off the raid.

Morgan came to the rescue again, at Hill's request, and bought enough NP voting stock to settle the issue for all time.

Yet, while this potent pair of buccaneers could defy Harriman, they were powerless to work their magic on the Supreme Court of the United States. A series of adverse lower-court decisions was finally upheld by the highest court in the land in a five-to-four decision handed down on March 4, 1904. Hill's brainchild was held to be illegal under terms of the Sherman Anti-Trust Act. So, from that point on, despite his significant holding in the NP, St. Paul's "Empire Builder" was unsuccessful in his desire to bend NP management to his will.[1]

Neither Hill's presence nor that of any of his friends and relatives had any impact on the dining car service. For that matter, in the years immediately following the bankruptcy, neither was it accorded much attention by any of the NP's top officers, beyond their making certain it would not deteriorate. In 1896 the dining car fleet stood at 25: a total of 27 cars had been purchased between 1883 and 1892, three had been destroyed by fires, and only one had been replaced; in 1892 two more were acquired from Barney & Smith. Not until 1902 did the company buy another, when it purchased four and ordered four more. All of these were intended for use in the consist of the new *North Coast Limited*, which had made its debut to the accompaniment of suitable fanfare on April 29, 1900.

Initially, this was planned as a summer tourist season train only, but its acceptance was so complete, and it so clearly dominated the field among all trains operating to the North Pacific coast, that NP executives agreed to let it become a year-round operation beginning May 5, 1901. Fee surely felt gratified at the success of his baby, but his claims for its equipment exaggerated the truth. An article in *Wonderland 1901*, a promotional booklet published annually by his department, said:

This train was the surprise of easterners, the pride of the Northern Pacific, and the talk of the West. It required ten distinct trains of eight cars each—eighty cars in all—to provide the necessary equipment, and nine of these trains were in synchronous operation a part of each day. The aggregate cost of these trains, each train being composed of new cars, was about $800,000, and each train weighed about 500 tons. The train is equipped with broad vestibules, Westinghouse air brakes, . . . steel platforms, M. C. B. couplers, Gold system of steam heat, electric lights, and steel-tired paper wheels.[2]

The facts tell another story. In the annual report for fiscal 1900, Second Vice President J. W. Kendrick wrote:

It having been decided to inaugurate limited transcontinental train service during the spring of 1900, it was necessary to prepare cars, and 95 cars of various classes were painted and varnished, furnished with electric wiring and fixtures, and 77 cars were equipped with steam heat at Como shops.

Passenger equipment was increased during the year by the purchase of 10 baggage and 10 tourist cars and 10 buffet observation cars.

Forty-seven cars of various classes were equipped with wide vestibules and steel platforms.

Forty-nine cars were equipped with National and 171 with M. C. B. couplers.

The electric lighting of Limited trains was accomplished by the installation of connected engine and generator of 35 horse power in each baggage car, with sufficient capacity to furnish ample current for 12-car train. All except baggage, express and mail cars . . . [have] storage batteries of sufficient capacity to light the trains at division points during exchange of engines.

Some of the equipment, like the observation-club cars, was new. Nothing like them had ever been seen west of the Mississippi on any railroad. They are credited with having introduced barber shop-valet service, baths, steam heat, electric lighting, and other travel frills to the West. Each had smoking and card rooms, tubs with showers, and a library boasting 140 volumes of the very latest in fiction and nonfiction, in addition to all popular magazines of the day.

Tourist sleepers with 16 sections were rather an oddity for a "limited." The cost of space was less than half that of a standard Pullman berth. Yet seats were upholstered in olive-green leather, and mahogany woodwork dominated. At one end of the car was a range for use by those who wished to cook their own meals. That seemed to be a holdover from Villard's emigrant sleepers. But on the new train, the bedding was standard Pullman issue, and it came with the space, a fact that Fee was quick to point out in his glowing descriptions.

Motive power for the luxury train was not fresh from the factory either. Its locomotives were 4-6-0 types, known everywhere as 10-wheelers, that had been built and delivered by Schenectady and the American Locomotive Company between 1893 and 1898 and redesignated from higher numbers to between 229 and 300. How many were actually assigned to the train is a matter of conjecture. Given the "exchange of engines" at each division point referred to by Kendrick, there had to be a minimum of 70. It was not a matter of concern to Fee. Passengers didn't ride in locomotives, did they?

The dining car service itself had become of less concern to him, well in advance of the *North Coast Limited*'s debut. Late in 1898, Tourtelot's area of responsibility had been given back to the operating department, removing it forever from the care of the passenger department and its advertising wing. The move had no effect on menus or service. Fee, a man of rather unremarkable stature who

Hazen J. Titus

affected a carefully groomed moustache as his only prominent descriptive, was content to carry on what had become
traditional, rather than introduce new dishes or modes of
service that would tend to show the company as a leader in
the field. It seems that to his mind, change and novelty
belonged to that part of the passenger business that would
bring an increase in patronage and swell the coffers of the
passenger department. Once the customer was on the
train, one had only to set a decent table and that patron
was a customer forever.

Tourtelot was a nose-to-the-grindstone, don't-run-
through-the-switch sort of dining car superintendent.
Chances are he felt he owed Fee his job and did not want
to seem ungrateful; in any case, he did nothing to make
Fee consider him a threat. Even after Fee's departure in
1904, the man did nothing to distinguish the NP from any
other high-class outfit. Food was good, service was above

Silent-screen movie star Ben Turpin, famous for
his crossed eyes, posed at the Seattle
commissary with an unidentified woman and
Dining Car Superintendent L. K. Owen, 1923.

average, and that was enough. There was little prospect for
change under his leadership. Following Tourtelot's death
in the spring of 1908, F. N. Finch, one of his assistants, was
appointed acting superintendent.

Under Finch's successor, who may well have been the
country's most creative dining car superintendent of all
time, innovation became the order of the day. Sometime
between Thanksgiving and Christmas, the name of Hazen
J. Titus began appearing in letters and print ads as NP
superintendent of dining cars. Soon thereafter, Titus set
out on a familiarization trip over the line that would
include a visit to the Seattle commissary, which had
become virtually an autonomous operation.

En route aboard the *North Coast Limited,* something
happened that would change Northern Pacific's image and
the reputation of its dining car department for the next six
decades. Titus overheard a conversation between two
Columbia Basin farmers who were lamenting the size of
potatoes harvested on their farms in the Yakima Valley.
He could not believe what he heard. The potatoes were
gigantic specimens, reaching as much as five pounds each.
Engaging the disappointed growers in conversation, he
learned they had tried to market their produce but had
found no takers. Most homemakers were unimpressed with
the tubers' incredible size and rather rough appearance.
Those who had ventured to cook them declared they were
inedible. They continued, then, to prefer smaller, more
delicate spuds that could be easily baked, boiled, or fried.
All that was left for the producers was to feed them to their
hogs, as European farmers did. But it struck Titus that
there had to be a way to capitalize on such anomalies.

Detraining with the growers at Yakima, he obtained a
large box of the potatoes and carried them to Seattle. At
the commissary he experimented for several days, produc-
ing results that both excited and inspired him. The potato
proved to be perfectly suited to baking. A two-pounder
baked for as long as two hours came from the oven snowy
white, tender, and mealy. Gently rolled to loosen the skin,
split lengthwise and drenched in butter, this natural

wonder possessed a flavor that was superior to the best baking potatoes of the day, including the vaunted Idaho russet. This was no too-hasty conclusion; Titus was a student of foodstuff and its history.[3]

Upon his return to St. Paul, probably in late December, Titus ordered all the potatoes the growers could produce that did not exceed two pounds each. Then, following delivery of the first batch of "Netted Gem Bakers," this specialty appeared on Northern Pacific menus and was served for the first time on February 9, 1909, to an unknown diner on the *North Coast Limited* who had dared to order it at a cost of 10 cents. Not only in the Columbia Basin, but throughout the country, potato growers might well have voted an award for Titus. The attention he focused on their crop increased use and sales everywhere.

But Titus did not pause to savor an isolated success. That year he introduced the NP's famous individual lemon pie, its Big Baked Apple, and a prize-winning fruit cake.

The dining car department produced booklets extolling the nutritional value of Washington apples and displayed them in its Chicago ticket office, 1927.

To find the latter, this king among dining car superinten-dents brought to the railroad that prince of master bakers, Frederick Kaul, who had a recipe for the brightest star in the fruit-cake firmament. No record exists to reveal how he came by the formula, but perhaps its source is less important than its history. The recipe had won a gold medal at the London Caterer's Exposition of 1873 and the *grand prix* in its class at the 1889 world's fair in Paris.

Menu entries that became specialties in a different way were products of the territory served by the railroad. Titus used them both to support area economies and to endow dining car patrons with a special feeling for the land they traversed. Potatoes and apples from Washington were just the beginning. In addition, he began featuring fresh fish, dairy products, and spring water from Minnesota; breads made from North Dakota wheat; beers brewed with that state's barley and Washington hops; beef, buffalo, and Rocky Mountain trout from Montana; Oregon prunes; Washington clams and salmon; and crab and reindeer from Alaska. And before quality control over the less exotic

Fred Kaul at the oven and his helpers in the Seattle commissary's bake shop, 1923

produce of NP territory could become a problem, he elected to grow it himself.

In 1909, the railroad began operating a 52-acre dairy and poultry farm, along with a hog farm, 17 miles east of Seattle in Washington's Kent Valley. Here, too, he was innovative. Eggs, produced at an average rate of 150 dozen each day, were dated almost as soon as they were laid, so that none would be used beyond their time. So were the caps on cream and milk bottles. Broiler chickens had to scale between 21 and 25 pounds per dozen. Swine were bred to produce lean, meaty specimens, long before fat and cholesterol became dietary scare words. He even decreed the exclusive use of pure, unsalted butter, purchased regularly from the Yakima Valley Creamery. Unhappily, his faith in this company was not entirely justified, and 18 months later he instituted the practice of churning butter daily, before dawn, on each dining car.

For a pamphlet issued by the passenger department in 1909, Titus contributed information about the new farms, as well as a typically understated comment about the food service it provided:

> *Dining cars, of unusually attractive design, add greatly to the transcontinental trip on the Northern Pacific. All meals are served at hours satisfactorily arranged to meet the wants of every patron.*
>
> *Every effort is exerted in the cooking and the serving to insure and maintain that uniform standard of excellence which is already a striking characteristic of Northern Pacific service.[4]*

In 1910, NP passenger revenues reached $21,333,000 a total that would be exceeded only once, in 1944. The total of 9,640,000 passengers that same year was also surpassed only once, in 1914, when 220,000 more travelers queued up at its ticket windows.[5]

Food service revenues, however, did not follow the trend of passenger travel. For example, in 1920, when passenger revenue nearly reached its 1910 level, dining and buffet car revenues, as well as those from hotels and restaurants, reached a new high. Then, passenger revenue began a rapid decline, falling to some $10 million for fiscal 1927-28. In that same period, food service revenues fell only slightly during the first two years, then leveled off, then rose again. In fiscal 1927-28, dining and buffet car revenue was $624,523 compared to $592,925 for 1921-22. Similarly, hotels and restaurants grossed $765,874 during 1927-28, but $724,395 in fiscal 1920-21.

Hotel and restaurant food service income in fact, always exceeded that of dining and buffet car service, and almost always showed a profit at year's end. From 1920 to 1941, dining car losses ranged between 24 and 40 percent, while hotels and restaurants lost money in only five years, and never more than 2.7 percent. Profits for the latter fluctuated between 1 and 8.3 percent. In those 22 years, dining cars lost $4,842,613 but hotels and restaurants made $488,380. This was one of several reasons the NP stayed in the restaurant trade, even if no attempt was made to match the quality of food and service offered on the trains.

Titus allowed himself to boast a bit in a 1911 handbook that described the *North Coast Limited* for prospective patrons:

> *The Northern Pacific has unusual facilities for supplying edibles to its dining cars. A 52-acre poultry farm at Kent, Wash. . . . affords the supply of fresh eggs. Each egg is stamped N.P.R.P.&D.F., meaning "Northern Pacific Railway Poultry and Dairy Farm." The dairy farm, with 300 thoroughbred milch cows, provides the milk and cream supply, which is constantly inspected and tested.*
>
> *This season an extensive truck garden is being laid out at Paradise, Montana, to supply vegetable products for the service. Large bakeries in Seattle and St. Paul, operated by the company, furnish all the bread, cake, pies and French pastry. The butter used*

A cake created by Kaul to celebrate the completion of the NP's Bitterroot branch line change, 1928

is unsalted. . . . *Wrappings of oiled paper protect it from contamination. The bread is also wrapped in tissue until cut for the table.*

A specialty is made of the Northern Pacific GREAT BIG BAKED POTATOES, which are unusually large and are selected because of their size and quality. The drinking water served is from the Pokegama Springs at Detroit, Minnesota. It is filtered and bottled at the springs. Afternoon tea with fruit cake, is served gratuitously upon request, to standard sleeping car patrons on all five transcontinental trains. Haviland china, decorated with a dainty Scotch thistle design, is used on all Northern Pacific dining cars. The silverware is of attractive design, bearing a special monogram.[6]

The casual mention of five transcontinental trains was another NP exaggeration, perhaps used to be prepared for such growth. In the summer of 1909 there were four such trains: one pair of NP "transcontinentals" ran between St. Paul and Billings. Another was the *Exposition Special*, operated that year from the last week of June to the third week of October for the Yukon-Pacific Exposition, held in Seattle. The railroad was, however, operating at record

ABOVE: Golden Guernsey dairy cows provided rich milk, cream, and butter.
OPPOSITE: The NP farm near Kent, Washington, 1916
LEFT: Chickens scratched and strolled among the farm's fenced runs.

ABOVE: Great Big Baked Potato
letter opener and spoon
OPPOSITE: Seattle commissary, 1923

levels, and all those trains meant the company needed a huge fleet of dining cars. Their numbers grew steadily from 25 in 1900, when the *North Coast Limited* was introduced, to 64 in 1915 (see table). That was the greatest number ever reached in the railroad's history.

In the meantime, too, the GREAT BIG BAKED POTATO came into its own as a promoter's dream. Encouraged by the spud's growing popularity among his patrons, Titus based an advertising campaign on it, ordering "potato premiums" to boost his road's food service. He came up with silver-plated spoons, letter openers, inkwells, blotters, lucky medallions, mechanical pencils, suede pennants, statuettes, aprons, sheet music, menus, and a platoon of postcards, all of which featured a giant tuber split down the middle, crowned with a huge pat of butter, and served with a large spoon. He organized the "Great Big Baked Potato Booster Club" and enrolled as members all dining car patrons who complimented the food or service. Each received a certificate of membership, made to look official and important by script and a scrollwork border, plus one of the silver spoons, which were produced by Wallace, the same firm that supplied the company's monogrammed tableware and plated serving pieces at that time.

NORTHERN PACIFIC DINING CARS, 1900-15

Date	Added	Retired	In Service
1900			25
1904	8		33
1906	12		45
1908	8		53
1909		6	47
1910	10		57
1911	4		61
1915	6	3	64

Source: NP, Annual Reports, 1900-16

Most monumental of all his potato souvenirs was a model that caught the eye of a *Railway Age Gazette* reporter. This item appeared in the issue of July 3, 1914:

> *The Northern Pacific has just finished at Seattle a new commissary building. With equipment it has cost approximately $30,000. A large trade mark, in the shape of a baked potato, 40 ft. long and 18 ft. in diameter, surmounts the roof. The potato is electric lighted and its eyes, through the electric mechanism, are made to wink constantly. A cube of butter thrust into its split top glows intermittently. The potato can be seen from the windows of all transcontinental trains entering Seattle.*

The new building—actually, an addition to the existing commissary—was just one of countless projects that gave testimony to the unprecedented growth in NP passenger business. Constructing a rail line across nearly 2,000 miles of uncultivated, townless wilderness, the NP had been forced to provide accommodations for its patrons from the beginning. Many frame structures sprang up in the wake of laboring tracklayers. Later inns were far more luxurious: The Portland, in Portland; The Tacoma, in Tacoma; The Manitoba, at Winnipeg; The Albemarle, at Helena. Others were rather more rustic, having been built to attract the intrepid outdoorsman, especially hunting and fishing tourists. Such were the Mountain House, in the Rockies at Heron, Montana, and the Highland House, at Hope, Idaho.

From the beginning, too, the railroad played a leading role in operating hotels and transportation facilities in Yellowstone National Park. For 18 years, Yellowstone reigned as the only national park in the land, and for many more years, the Northern Pacific was the sole common carrier to provide access to its wonders. With no other corporate entity in the vicinity, it fell naturally to the

railroad to assume a position of leadership in offering hotel and coach services.

Between 1901 and 1910, 18 passenger depots and two restaurant buildings were erected across the system, all but one going up at major main-line points. All were of brick construction, except the poured-concrete depot at Bismarck, North Dakota. And those at Missoula, Montana, and Wallace, Idaho, owed something to the dining car department: the bricks used in them had been imported from China expressly for construction of a luxury hotel at Tacoma. Advance publicity for the NP's new Olympic Hotel, named in 1890 for the range of mountains west of Puget Sound, had compared it favorably with such world famous hostelries as Shepheards of Cairo, The Raffles in Singapore, and Quebec City's Chateau Frontenac. Unfortunately, no one ever learned if such comparisons were valid; the hotel never opened for business. It was completed except for the interior finish when the NP went into receivership in 1893.

After a fire gutted the structure in 1899, the shell was partially dismantled, and many of the bricks were used to face the new depot and division headquarters building at Missoula and the chateaulike passenger station at Wallace. In 1904, the Olympic's remains were sold to the city of Tacoma, for use in the construction of a high school. Thus ended the NP's dream of a chain of luxury hotels linking Lake Superior with Puget Sound. Of course, those the company still owned continued to be operated under the dining car department.

Despite the NP's large showing at the outset, it never rivaled European and Canadian lines in hotel ownership and operation. By 1918, the railroad had evidently sold all interest in its hotels, but it retained ownership of its depot restaurants—lunch counters and lunchrooms in dining car parlance. These, too, were thinned as time passed. From a commanding position of almost total dominance in the field, the NP's involvement in feeding and housing passengers had vastly diminished by the 1920s.[7]

The NP's dining car service was made a true island in this stream, cut off from the mainland but never out of sight, almost from its birth in 1883. Little that went on in the surrounding world directly affected its people or its mode of operations, even when the company suffered financial reverses. In the days following the bankruptcy of 1893, it continued to enjoy the good reputation it had earned when skies were bluer.

Early in 1894, E. B. Northrop, a Minnesota travel writer, made a reconnaissance that began in St. Paul and took him south to Dallas and Fort Worth, then west over the lines of a number of the NP's rivals. Smalley carried an account of his trip in the May 1894 issue of *The Northwest*. Northrop learned first hand just how well the NP was doing and ate a little crow as a consequence:

At Fort Worth we had our first experience with the eating stations which the Texas Pacific, the Southern Pacific, and the Central and Union Pacific permit to do business along their lines. After two or three attempts to eat some of the filthy, miserable meals placed before us at these "dining rooms," . . . I thought, with regrets I am unable to express, of having once said that the service on a certain Northern Pacific dining car might have been somewhat improved.

It may be of interest to the management of the N. P. dining car system to learn that there were quite a number of ladies and gentlemen on the train that carried us over the Texas Pacific and thence over the Southern Pacific, who were familiar with the Northern Pacific, and a considerable portion of their conversation was at times devoted to lamentations that they were debarred the privileges of "a nice, clean meal in an N. P. dining car." So far as the general make-up of the trains was concerned, the condition of the track, roadbed and everything that goes to make up a railway system, from Dallas to El Paso and thence to San Francisco, it may be all that the greater portion

of that country is worthy of; but compared with the system and service of the Northern Pacific and its splendid (I was not so sure of their splendor before) vestibuled trains, I have no words adequate to decry the former and praise the latter. . . . The N.P. may have used lots of money to bring its system and service up to its present standard, but it is something every bond-holder and stockholder ought to rejoice at, even if the company is a "little behind the light-house."

Thus it went, year after year. Major concussions in the world and within the ranks were little more than ripples in the stream for the men who worked under Tourtelot and, later, Titus. Out went the Northern Pacific Railroad and in came the Northern Pacific Railway; Morgan supplanted Villard as the keeper of the purse strings; a war with Spain excited the general populace but it neither provoked a quiver of anticipation nor added a discernible farthing to the NP's bottom line. The U.S. Supreme Court ruled against the Northern Securities Company, and James J. Hill and E. H. Harriman made their cameo appearances, all small potatoes compared to Irish linen and French china. In the meantime, Titus entered stage right and did much to solidify the NP's position among the best passenger railroads in the world.

Permanent and substantial commissaries established by Titus in St. Paul and Seattle brought a stability to operations of the department that was welcomed by those who followed in his footsteps. He made the stocking of cars at those stations into a science and saved money by reducing en-route purchases at higher cost. Top management came to respect his expertise and left him to operate without interference. Lunchrooms, maligned everywhere else in the country, became a matter of pride to the department and the company. Titus placed them under the supervision of experienced and locally known food purveyors only, then policed them with an assiduousness that offended

none and earned him their respect. His attitude toward crews on his dining cars was paternal yet pedagogical.

NP stewards were trained as friendly *maîtres d'hôtels*, as well as humanitarian supervisors; cooks were taught to prepare meals as though their lives, as well as their jobs, depended on it; and the waiters learned to serve those meals to the complete satisfaction of the patron. Nothing else much mattered. All went well until Congress declared war on Germany on April 6, 1917.

The events leading up to war had made virtually no impression on rail managements in their pursuit of profits, but White House pragmatists judged that U.S. railroads would not cooperate sufficiently with each other and the government. (The railroads were evidently expected to *act* like lovers, but were not permitted to consummate their relationships in mergers.) Consequently, President Woodrow Wilson and his congressional allies devised a "stand-by" law empowering the chief executive to take over the railroad industry in a national emergency. According to NP President Jule M. Hannaford, on December 1 the Interstate Commerce Commission (ICC) had "commended the operations of railroads in their efforts to act as a unit."[8] Four weeks later, on December 28, 1917, President Wilson issued a proclamation taking over the railroads.

The industry had put together a plan for coordinated operations during several months of meetings in Washington. Even the ICC expressed the view that the necessary unification of rail operations could be achieved if federal restrictions were eased. But there were problems with congestion, and each branch of the military establishment made chaos out of orderliness by demanding preferential treatment.

Significantly, the government had left control of troop movements in hands experienced in passenger service—the industry itself. P. Harvey Middleton, secretary of the Railway Business Association, noted in 1941 that "the railways, in addition to the traffic arising from the current demands of our population, were called upon to carry, in the period of June 1917 to June 1919, some 13,000,000 military passengers." With that performance in mind, M. J. Gormley, executive assistant for the Association of American Railroads, took a jaundiced view of the government's ineptness in the business of shipping war materiel and necessary civilian freight:

> *The story with reference to freight movement is different and not at all satisfactory. The difficulty was caused by there being no coordination between the different branches of the government, by permitting cars to be loaded when there was no place to unload them and thereby blocking port and other facilities. I think this is best demonstrated by the record, which shows that at one time there were over 200,000 cars under load and standing still that could not be moved because . . . there was no place to unload them.*[9]

This experiment in nationalization proved to be a costly lesson for the country. The NP's experience was typical among western lines.

In 1916, the company's rail operations brought in a record $80.3 million; expenses came to $43.2 million; and total operating income, after taxes, reached $31.5 million, the highest level in company history. In contrast, although railway operating revenues in 1920 soared 40 percent to $113 million, expenditures (many required by the government) rose more than 233 percent to $101 million. So, after paying $10 million in taxes, the NP was left with operating income of just under $2 million.

Based on the government's surety against loss, then, the company should have been reimbursed a minimum of $40 million by the end of 1920. Profitability aside, this was barely enough to meet the increased cost of labor, which rose from $28.2 million in 1916 to an astounding $66.5

million in 1920. On July 20 that year, the U.S. Labor Board rendered "Wage Decision No. 2," effective May 1, "under which wages for all employees covered by working agreements and properly before the Board, were granted substantial increases in rates of pay." And, added the NP's new president, Charles Donnelly, in a statement cosigned with Chairman Howard Elliott for the company's 1920 annual report, "It was necessary to grant similar increases to employees not before the board. These increases amounted in all to $11,200,000 per annum." In other words, dining car crews were among the beneficiaries.

If rail management tended to see reform politicians and labor leaders of the day as dreamers living in a state of confused and confusing ecstasy, they had a measure of justification on their side. The uncontrolled surge in expenses seemed to spring from labor's and government's apparently shared belief that rail coffers were bottomless pits of gold, there to be mined at will.

In 1916 Congress had passed and Wilson had signed a bill that became known as the Adamson Law. Under the guise of establishing the principle of eight-hour workdays for all of America, it served to forestall a nationwide railroad strike by giving operating union members a handsome increase in wages. This was possible because they were not paid by the hour but received a daily wage, calculated by a complex "time/mileage" formula.

In any other business, these added costs could be passed on to consumers by raising prices. Regulated as they were, railroads could only apply for rate increases, to both the ICC and the state railroad commissions, a time-consuming procedure that militated against quick recovery of expenses and rarely produced the desired result. Under government control during the war, rates went up, but nowhere near enough to match soaring wage scales.

The wage scale for dining car waiters, all of whom were black, provides an informative comparison. Waiters, whether black or white, can never be said to have been overpaid at any time in their history. Employers, it has seemed, have tended to think of them as vendors of a service for which patrons were expected to pay by means of a gratuity. The nominal wage paid is not intended to equal more than half a living wage. To a limited degree, this may be considered an apt concept. As a rule, conscientious servers can expect to be paid (rewarded, in the minds of some) with a handsome tip. Only the big tippers, however, could ever calculate a waiter's monthly tip income as anything but modest.

According to William F. Paar, who entered the NP's dining car service in 1912 and served as superintendent from 1948 to 1968, waiters were paid about $15 and earned an estimated $10 to $15 in tips each month at the turn of the century. At the end of 1915, the company's 125 waiters received $25 per month, and Paar assumed that tip income had kept pace. By the time the U.S. Railroad Administration (USRA) took command at the beginning of 1918, the NP had raised the waiters' basic rate by 10 percent to $27.50. (During that period, stewards with the most seniority received an increase from $95 to $100 per month, a bit more than 5 percent.)[10]

When the government intervened, however, it went all the way. General Order No. 27 of the USRA dealt with wages, hours, and working conditions and covered all railway employees, both operating and nonoperating,

union and nonunion. Out of it came wage increases in the range of $45 per month for NP dining car stewards and $27.50 for the waiters. Thus, the latter were blessed in 1918 with a doubling of their wages, even though they belonged to no union. (On the other hand, they received some benefits from union negotiations: NP stewards were organized, and company policy held that "rules affecting hours of service and over-time . . . applied to the [dining car] crew as a unit.")[11]

As good as it was, it got even better. On November 30, 1920, there were 120 NP waiters, and each was paid $81.52 per month. The railroad's annual cost for dining car waiters had risen in five years by 213 percent, from $37,500 to nearly $117,400. Lest anyone think there was bias toward white employees at the expense of black, it must be noted that in 1918 the NP's third cooks, all of whom were white, received $27.50 per month, the same base rate as waiters; a small group of them received $32.50 per month by reason of greater experience and seniority. In 1918 the USRA raised the base rate to $32.50—but third cooks could earn no tips. Therefore, waiters enjoyed higher income each month than was possible for even the best-paid third cook. But if the rest of the nation would look back on the decade of the twenties and say they roared, the NP's nonunion blacks would be exaggerating if they said those years produced for them anything louder than a murmur.[12]

Waiters and Unions

*A*LTHOUGH *NONUNION RAILROAD* employees fared better financially under government control of the industry, they were among the first to sacrifice some of their gains when the high-flying passenger business began to lose altitude after 1920. Large wage increases granted by the U.S. Railway Labor Board that year were short-lived for all but the "ops," or operating employees—those who worked on the trains. In 1921, "non-ops" on the nation's railroads took cuts of more than 10 percent, then a year later lost most of what remained of those increases.[1]

A mini-depression that hit the United States late in 1920 and carried well into the next year brought on the wage reductions. Passenger income reached $21.1 million in 1920, just short of the record set in 1914, then began to decline with the relentless expansion of automobile production and ownership. Although NP freight revenues rebounded encouragingly in 1922, passenger revenues continued to fall for decades, until World War II gas rationing sent Americans scurrying back to depot ticket counters.

During those years, the dining car waiters, buffet car porters, observation car porters, and train porters set out to organize themselves into a collective bargaining unit. (The dining car waiters had been covered by NP labor agreements that applied to stewards and cooks, as well.) However, because of the workers' lack of experience in organizing, their early efforts were only partially successful. The Northern Pacific's operating department officers were old hands at dealing with union organizers. Early in September 1924, A. W. (Alec) Thomson, the new superintendent of dining cars, received a letter from Minneapolis attorney Glesner R. Fowler, who claimed to be general chairman of St. Paul's embryonic Brotherhood of Sleeping and Dining Car Employees Union. The letter, addressed simply and inaccurately to "Mr. Thompson," requested a conference to discuss a proposed agreement. NP officials were suspicious. Not one of the officers listed

on the brotherhood's letterhead was employed by the NP, and Fowler offered no evidence that his group truly represented a majority of the NP's waiters and porters. Furthermore, Fowler's double gaffe in addressing the letter cast doubt on his knowledge of the company and its employee relations. Thomson conducted an informal poll among some of his employees and found only one observation car porter who said he was a dues-paying member of the brotherhood. The railroad's officers, convinced that Fowler did not represent over half the employees and thus had no legal standing, ignored his request.[2]

On December 11, Fowler wrote again, this time to Vice President John M. Rapelje. Rapelje, in turn, referred the letter to his assistant, Samuel A. Wilder, the NP's negotiating chief. Wilder's first act was to ask Thomson to make a more precise determination of union membership among the NP's waiters and porters. The superintendent reported that of the 80 he polled, only five claimed to belong to Fowler's organization. Once more, no response was given to the letter.[3]

On January 26, 1925, the patient Fowler wrote another letter. Aiming as high as possible, he sent it to Charles Donnelly, the NP's president, who forwarded it to Aaron M. Burt, successor to Rapelje, who had died suddenly on January 20. Burt relayed the letter to Wilder and asked for an explanation. The latter replied on February 9, admitting that the labor relations department had paid no attention to Fowler's communications and summing up the reasons for that decision:

> *Until such time as Mr. Fowler produces evidence that his Organization does represent 51% of these employes* [sic] *and that they desire an agreement with the Northern Pacific Railway Company we of course will not negotiate with his Organization, and it is presumptious* [sic] *on his part to write us if he does not represent the majority of these employes, and our*

OPPOSITE: Waiters and a steward on the *Yellowstone Comet*, 1925

information indicates that he represents only 5 out of 80. However, I presume he is entitled to the courtesy of a reply.[4]

In addition, Wilder noted that Fowler, who was black, evidently represented the black employees of the Great Northern; but since the Northern Pacific's agreements were applied to *all* dining car employees, regardless of race, the managers felt that his questions did not apply.

In his suggested reply, Wilder showed he would give Fowler no room to maneuver, no hope of achieving his goal of obtaining a contract with the NP. In fact, Wilder wanted Donnelly to say he was sure the NP's waiters and porters had no desire to be represented by the brotherhood. Three days later, the president wrote to Fowler, but only to say he had referred the matter to the operating vice president. On February 14 Burt responded, using Wilder's suggestion. But Fowler could not be brushed off so easily, and he tried to make his next move a decisive one. He filed a complaint with the U.S. Railroad Labor Board, which had been created under the Transportation Act of 1920. It was very nearly his last official act before he quietly disappeared from the scene.[5]

Although Fowler's motives were questionable and his actions were sometimes baffling, his tactics might have paid off had he followed the rules. But he was prone to error and, in the end, his involvement only prolonged the black employees' fight to achieve a collective bargaining agreement. The NP, itself, eventually opened the door to success.

"General chairman" Fowler's machinations had confused the Labor Board to the point that it scheduled a conference in Chicago on July 1 just to sort out the claims and counterclaims. Fowler attended this meeting, but the chief NP employee delegate was Cleat W. Oliver, one of the five avowed NP members of the union, whose name had suddenly appeared on the letterhead as president of

the brotherhood during the protracted sparring. Unfortunately, Oliver and his colleagues were unable to produce a list of bona fide signatures or any other evidence to show that the organization had been designated by 51 percent of the NP's waiters and porters as their bargaining unit. There was nothing the board could do but disclaim jurisdiction. At the same time, its chairman arrogated to himself the right to make a ruling in the case anyway. Nearly five months elapsed before Decision No. 3971 was handed down. In it, after noting that "the representative of the carrier [Wilder] stated that he was willing to meet in conference a committee of employees on the question of representation and rules," he concluded:

> Decision.—*The Railroad Labor Board remands this dispute for conference between the representatives of the employees and the carrier for the purpose of negotiating an agreement. Should the question of representation arise, it shall be determined by secret ballot in the manner prescribed in [previous] Decisions.*[6]

Three weeks after the Chicago confrontation, and well before a formal decision could be announced, President Oliver and two other members of the brotherhood, William S. Butler and Henry J. Maxwell, asked for a meeting "to discuss . . . Wages and hours of service and . . . Other working conditions affecting our employment." Wilder demurred because he wanted more time to research other aspects of an agreement with the waiters and porters. On December 21, after the decision was announced, the two sides finally faced each other across a conference table, held inconclusive talks, and agreed to have another meeting after at least 30 days. In addition, the employee delegation learned that NP waiters were earning 60 cents per month more than their Great Northern counterparts, who already had a company-affiliated organization, and

that if an agreement were to be negotiated, "the Railway Company would feel justified in establishing similar rates for similar service on the Northern Pacific as is now paid on the Great Northern."[7]

Although the managers' threat of reduced wages was probably as idle as it was naked, novice negotiators could not be expected to know that. Wilder and company managers clearly preferred a company-sponsored employee organization, which would keep outside agitators out of future negotiations. At the next meeting, on March 6, 1926, the delegates proposed the option that was easiest for management to accept—an association that would be independent of any local or national labor union—and they requested that the company help formulate the

A waiter offered tray service, 1935.

fledgling union's constitution and bylaws. The rough drafts would be placed before the membership and voted on before the next meeting.[8]

Two months later, the representatives of the employees brought evidence that they represented the will of the majority. The waiters and porters, they said, would accept the proposed document if several changes were made: dues would be set at 50 cents per month instead of 25 cents; train porters and train maids would be included; and a clause would be inserted that called for a board of adjustment composed of three union members and three NP representatives. This body would have the authority "to hear and decide such matters as under the agreement creating the said board of adjustment may be referred to it." All these changes were acceptable to the NP.[9]

Perhaps the most significant part of the constitution from the railroad's point of view was a provision inserted by Wilder that was designed to assure the company it could retain some degree of control over the group. Article 9 stipulated that "Members of this association shall not join any other trade union, association or like organization covering the same kind of work as that performed by the members of this association, where such union, association or organization obligations in any manner conflict with this constitution. . . . This association shall not join, affiliate, amalgamate or cooperate with any other organization or association."[10]

The "Constitution of the Association of Dining Car Waiters and Porters—Northern Pacific Railway Company" was ratified by both parties in September and took effect October 1, 1926. Thereafter, a decade of relative calm followed, during which the name of the so-called union was changed to "Northern Pacific Waiters and Porters Protective Association." More importantly, the employees used the time to gain bargaining experience and sophistication. With these came increased familiarity with labor law, under the aegis of which they were able to move confidently to achieve affiliation with the American Federation of Labor (AFL).

When the NP signed an agreement on November 22, 1938, it revealed it was ready, at last, to recognize the right of the newly formed and independent Dining Car Employees Union, Local No. 516, to bargain collectively for the black employees. On that day, too, the pioneer Protective Association ceased to exist. This new accord was limited to that single issue and had no effect on rates of pay, although the president of the local, Maceo A. Finney, had reported that the group sought a 20 percent increase. A progressive wage scale, negotiated in 1936, represented a

ceiling that NP management said it was unable to breach until the decline in revenues and net income could be reversed. The organization accepted this explanation without argument. By terms of that two-year-old agreement, base pay ranged from $72 per month for entry-level waiters up to $96 for those with 15 or more years of service with Northern Pacific. In any case, bargaining must have been conducted amiably both before and after the waiters and porters became part of the AFL. Not once in the history of the NP's dining car service was there ever a serious threat of a strike, and there is no record that the question ever was put to a vote.[11]

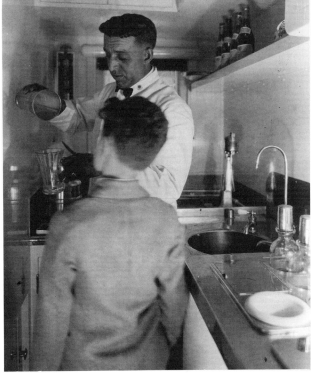

C. L. McCullough, hairdresser on the 1930 *North Coast Limited,* also provided soda fountain service from a small but well-equipped galley.

At the request of a stewardess-nurse, a chef pours warm formula into a nursing bottle, 1962.

NP management's pursuit of profits was invested with the same moral and ethical certainty that distinguished its approach to labor relations. Orthodoxy decreed that each part of the whole must be profitable, as well as the sum of those parts. As a rule, then, any person or operation that failed to contribute to the supreme goal, or that detracted from it needlessly, was regarded as expendable. Except, that is, for the dining car service. From Villard to Donnelly there had existed that anomalous tenet of the NP's creed: dining cars lose money, but they function both as a showcase and as an answer to a human need over long distances and must be operated as such. In this respect, the NP outshone most other lines, whose top officials begrudged the loss of a lone cent but who knew full well that their failure to provide on-train food service might result in even greater losses. Although all gave in to the demand, the efforts of most to minimize dining car deficits led them to condone meals and service that fell well below the high level of quality that long had been standard on the Northern Pacific.

Throughout the 1920s and 1930s, the NP tried to maintain that level while holding the line on food prices. As the depression intensified and patronage fell off, however, reductions had to come. Some of the more elaborate meals disappeared from menus, and less expensive ingredients were substituted in many recipes to cut costs and to make them seem more like "home-style" cooking. On the other hand, crew size remained intact, except on the *Yellowstone Comet*. This was an all-Pullman, transcontinental train that provided direct service to Yellowstone National Park. (Actually, one set of trains operated between Chicago and Gardiner, Mont., northern gateway to the park, and another between Seattle and Gardiner.)

In 1927, after passenger revenues seemed to have settled into an irreversible slide, Thomson took an innovative step that could have altered the face of dining car service for all time. He assigned a crew of six women to serve patrons on Comet dining cars, hoping to lure passengers away from other railroads, especially close rivals like the Great Northern and the Milwaukee. Soon he was forced to raise the complement to eight, in order for the women to serve tables at the same pace as six men without being overtaken by fatigue. Men seemed better able to withstand the grind of 14-hour days. Unfortunately, the expense of two additional crew members was not justified by a sufficient increase in patronage, so the precedent-shattering experiment was terminated in 1930. Thomson's novel idea became one of the victims of cutback fever, and diner guests on the main line never experienced the astonishment of being served by waitresses. This was the only instance in which women were employed in dining cars, although maids and beauticians had a long history of working on NP trains, and a capable stewardess-nurse graced each run of the Vista-Dome *North Coast Limited* from 1955 to 1970.[12]

From 1920 to 1940, the railroad industry fought wars on two different fronts. Autos and paved highways put the traveler in the driver's seat, giving railroads a bad case of financial malnutrition long before the country caught the depression bug. By 1929 rail travel losses had become a way of life on the high iron, and the official arrival of hard times only accelerated that decline. In 1933, NP passenger income fell to $3.2 million, the lowest since fiscal 1896-97.[13]

Even so, the NP was loath to retrench. The equipment roster testified to the upheaval in travel during that fateful period. The freight car fleet equipped to haul automobiles grew dramatically, from 925 in 1920 to 3,435 just 10 years later. Over the same decade, passenger traffic declined 84 percent—from 8.5 million to 1.4 million—but the company's passenger-carrying fleet was pared only from 636 to 482 cars. This reduction of 24 percent came nowhere near matching the loss of business, a sure sign that the NP did not consider the situation hopeless.

As usual, food service more than held its own, at least in terms of rolling stock and personnel. Although the roster of dining cars fell from 52 to 42 units in that period, the raw figures do not tell the whole story. In an effort to bring economy to the menu, the NP introduced a new type of car in 1928. Six first-class coaches were converted to café cars. Basically, they were half coach, half lunch counter. The menu was not unlike that used in the line's depot restaurants. Passengers could order anything from two doughnuts and a glass of water for a nickel to a complete plate dinner for 50 to 65 cents. This meal included beverage and dessert. Best of all, each of these cars could serve 18 guests at a single sitting, but was staffed by only two, a cook and the waiter-in-charge.

Gratified by patron response, management grew bolder. In mid-1929, before the smooth surface of Wall Street became a nightmare of sinkholes and dropoffs, the NP's board of directors approved orders for nine new dining cars to be delivered by May 1, 1930. Then, in 1931, six more coaches were remodeled into café cars. And in 1933, while passenger receipts were sinking to the very bottom of the pit, management gritted its collective teeth and ordered air conditioning for the entire fleet, beginning with the observation and dining cars on its premier train, the *North Coast Limited*. Of course, the work was done by company

forces at the NP's Como Shops in St. Paul, an economy measure that actually brought a small increase in employment for the city during the depression. It took seven years to do the work, but the expense was worth it, apparently. Passenger revenues began recovering in 1934 and rose 42 percent by 1937. Through it all, the dining cars lost money, as expected.

If top management lamented the sacrifice of $75,000 to $200,000 annually on the altar of passenger comfort, especially in a year such as 1932 when the company's total operations suffered a deficit of nearly $2 million, they never revealed it publicly. On the other hand, the dining car personnel neither regretted losing money nor suppressed their feelings about it. In fact, it was almost as though they believed they were not doing a good job unless the department operated at a loss. In 1963, while being interviewed for a story in *The Telltale*, an NP publication for employees, Superintendent Paar reported that he spent from $1.20 to $1.25 on food and labor for each $1 of dining car revenue. And he said it with something akin to pride in his voice. Then he added, "The only time we ever made any money was during World War II."[14] What he did not say was that the war provided the last hurrah for railroad passenger business and traditional dining car service.

Dining Car Line
to the Pacific

THOMSON AND HIS MINIONS in the dining car service did not suddenly set out to make money during the war. Profit was accidental, merely a by-product of efficiency and time-saving changes that enabled overworked crews and overtaxed space to accommodate record numbers of guests at each meal. Furthermore, the huge increase was not so much a matter of high passenger counts on the trains as it was the unheard-of percentage of travelers who patronized the dining cars.[1]

Troop train movements accounted for the greater part of wartime passenger traffic, of course, but they placed no demands on the NP's dining car service. Rolling stock, including kitchen cars, was owned by the government and by other railroads, and the carrier's own equipment rarely saw service in those trains. At the same time, regularly scheduled trains were patronized by military personnel traveling under orders both individually and in small groups, and all came armed with tickets redeemable for a dollar per meal per person. Then, too, men and women from all branches of the military traveled by train while on leave. Few of them ignored "mess call," even though they had to pay for it themselves. Moreover, a larger proportion of nonmilitary passengers were inclined to take their meals in dining cars than during peacetime, both because they were better able to afford it and because they could order meat and other foods that were rationed. Most rail travelers, in uniform or not, had money to spend for the first time in half a lifetime, and even if none took it seriously, they seemed to adopt the fatalist's philosophy of "Eat, drink, and be merry." What better place to apply it than on a train, traveling as they had fantasized—and what better time than while in full flight from a not-quite-forgotten depression, especially when there was a war on?

Challenged to meet the demands of vastly increased patronage, the NP dispensed with many of the frills on which the dining car service had built its reputation. Instead of full-service place settings, for example, each military passenger sat down to a meal served on a single plate with a knife, fork, and spoon. Doily underliners and finger bowls were shelved; menus were printed on recycled paper with no artwork except the Treasury Department's symbolic Minuteman, their advertising aimed only at exhorting the public to buy war bonds and to conserve food. Dining cars were opened for service an hour earlier, at 6:00 A.M., and GIs were called to meals before civilian travelers. Only a few of the latter found fault with a policy that most perceived as an acceptable sacrifice for "our boys in uniform," and once the malcontents were seated before a bountiful spread in the diner, all traces of resentment vanished.

Cooks and waiters worked longer hours than ever before, and the latter were pushed to the limit as they raced between the kitchen and their assigned tables, dodging each other and keeping up with the flood of orders. Of course, their runs had begun some hours before the scheduled departures of their assigned trains from St. Paul and Seattle, because the rolling restaurants had to be stocked with all the food, linens, china, silver, pots, pans, and other supplies that would sustain them for several days on the road. And at the commissaries, in the manner of their predecessors as far back as 1883, unsung car cleaners, butchers, bakers, and order takers performed their preparatory tasks long before the crews arrived to load up.

Determined to obtain the choicest cuts, buyers rose before dawn and scurried from one wholesale meat distributor to another in South St. Paul and Seattle—not to mention cities along the route where NP lunchrooms still provided food service for employees, town customers, and travelers—selecting their prime beef, pork, lamb, wild game, fish, and poultry. Soon after the chosen legs, loins, and racks were delivered, butchers trimmed the meat, divided it into roasts and individual serving portions, and sealed them in waxed parchment. Eastern and Great Lakes fish and seafoods were issued to cars at St. Paul, while those stocked at the Seattle commissary received Pacific Northwest salmon and shellfish from markets on

OVERLEAF: The westbound *North Coast Limited* at Billings, 1959, with Pullman cars parked directly in front of the depot, right. The lunchroom is to its left and the "Clark Fork River," a business car used by the NP's vice president for operations, is on the "house track" beyond it. OPPOSITE: Butcher shop of the Seattle commissary, 1923

OPPOSITE: The NP's streamlined *North Coast Limited* along the Jefferson River in Montana

the wharf. And, depending on which poultry dishes were to be featured on a week's menus, orders of duck, squab chicken, guinea hen, and turkey would be placed on board.

At the NP's bake shops, one at each end of the line, all breads, rolls, pastries, and pastas were made for the first day out. An abundance of the NP's special toast bread, baked two and a half pounds to the loaf, was stocked at the commissaries in a quantity sufficient to last for the entire run. Any other breads and rolls needed for the last leg of trips in either direction could be supplied freshly baked from the centrally located lunchroom at Livingston. Pies, puddings, and similar foods were made right on the cars for second and third days away from terminals. Salad dressings, sauces, soup stocks, and bouillons were prepared from scratch in the company's own kitchens, and the fresh fruits and vegetables (the orange juice was freshly squeezed every morning) were drawn from storage in large root cellars that hugged the basement walls of each commissary. In all, some one and a half tons of food went onto shelves and into bins of the pantry and coolers of an NP dining car. And that was just the edibles and potables.

China, silver, cooking utensils, and cleaning tools and powders usually remained on the cars, but stewards had to make end-of-run inventories so they could replace any broken, exhausted, or missing items and maintain everything at standard-issue levels. For those who stopped to wonder about it, a steward's success in placing so much on a car had to be either a major mystery or a minor miracle. If he was not born with resourcefulness, he quickly learned it.

One of those stewards was St. Paul native Bob Jones, who followed his future father-in-law, Roy Davis of Seattle, into the dining car service and began a 40-year career when he became a "jitney" in 1942. That entry-level position called for carrying sandwiches, beverages, fruit, and snack food through the train—sandwiches cost 10, 15, and 20 cents, pie was only a dime, milk cost a dime, and coffee was still just a nickel a cup—to accommodate the coach passengers who declined to use the dining car. After two trips, Bob became the sixth waiter in his crew, a man the others regarded as "mule" to the pantryman, the highest ranking of the six waiters assigned to each car. Some time later, Bob was promoted to waiter-in-charge and assigned either to a café car or a club car, where the staff—a cook or a counterman, and sometimes both—worked under his supervision. On this job he, like a steward, had to find a place for everything and keep everything in its place.

"We were always looking for more space," he recalled in 1985, noting that this was especially true when there was a large tour group on board and only one dining car. "For example, all the linens would be folded and put away as neatly as possible. That way the lockers would hold enough to get us all the way to Seattle."[2]

He was not referring to the 1,904 miles between St. Paul and the Seafair city; he meant the 2,766-mile run that included the eastward journey from St. Paul to Chicago, then back west to the shores of Puget Sound. When Bob joined the NP, that run took the *North Coast Limited* 73 hours and 30 minutes (including a layover of 12 hours and 15 minutes in Chicago). The *Alaskan*, the railway's No. 2 train and the one he was assigned to until after World War II, took nearly 24 hours more.

In addition to the pressures of having to carry sufficient stocks of comestibles, tableware, napery, and cookware during those years of peak usage, Supt. Thomson and his crews had to cope with food shortages. For example, while meat rationing did not directly affect the service, at times there just was not enough of it available to last through an entire trip. At first, this called for great ingenuity in putting together a set of menus for the week. After all, they had always been printed well in advance and were rotated regularly as a means of avoiding repetition. Later, basic menus were devised that could be used without trouble if they were augmented with tip-ons. These small squares of colored paper, attached to a menu by folds at the

A NEW HIGH
IN RAILROAD SERVICE

On this train, just ahead of the Dining Car, is the Lewis and Clark Traveller's Rest, a luxurious, new Buffet-Lounge car which, we sincerely believe, is the most interesting, attractive and serviceable passenger car of its kind on any American railroad. You'll know what we mean when you visit it. All passengers are invited to use its facilities. Outstanding service features of the Traveller's Rest are:

Meals—Breakfast, Luncheon and Dinner—In the Buffet section, with 14 comfortable leather-cushioned stools, select and a la carte meals and snacks at popular prices are served at the counter from 7 AM throughout the day.

Beverages—There's beverage service all day and evening in the Lounge section, where there are seats for 30 persons in comfortable upholstered sofas and chairs.

Library, Cards, Music—Also in the Lounge section there are magazines and tables for cards and throughout the Traveller's Rest car there is radio reception, and background music from the train's high fidelity sound system.

"History on Wheels"—Colorful historical murals and other fascinating exhibits depict the famous journey of the celebrated explorers, Lewis and Clark. Be sure to visit this unusual Traveller's Rest car—just ahead of the Dining Car.

G. W. Rodine,
Passenger Traffic Manager

Route of the Vista-Dome
North Coast Limited

F6926 4-'56

ABOVE: *Traveller's Rest* cars were
introduced in 1955.
OPPOSITE: Teen-aged employees had
many tasks, including keeping the
huge stocks of silver in a high state
of polish and neatly stored.

top edges, bore descriptions of various specials, such as tenderloin steak with mushroom caps. As long as there was a supply of steak on hand, a menu would appear with that tip-on. When no individual serving portion remained, the menu could still be used with a tip-on announcing a different special, such as roast prime rib of beef or Dungeness crab. This innovation was so successful it became departmental policy.[3]

Intermittent shortages were only momentary inconveniences, but there was one pair of wartime casualties that had a more profound effect on the dining car service. Patrons were quick to notice the disappearance of the NP's Great Big Baked Potato from their menus, but at least *it* would return when the war was over. On the other hand, a change in the quality of linens went virtually unnoticed by the average NP traveler, although dining car employees, gourmets, and aficionados of dining car linen recognized the difference and felt a grave sense of loss. For until 1941—no one now remembers when the practice was instituted—the railway had used only imported Irish linens on its tables. Tragically, in the opinion of Bill Paar, the ship that carried the replenishing supply to America was sunk by a U-boat attacking an impromptu convoy of merchantmen in the North Atlantic. As a consequence, after the existing supply had been worn until it almost defied description—more than 5.6 million meals were served in 1944 alone—a domestic source had to be found. Irish linen would never again be used on Northern Pacific dining cars.

But, then, the cars themselves were about to be scuttled, too. The effects of age and constant, excessive service had reduced the dining car fleet to 23 not-too-well-preserved specimens. No longer were they even a pale reflection of the NP's progressive attitude. Quite the contrary. None had been acquired since 1930, and the oldest ones had been delivered in 1906. The latter, although remodeled in 1924, were much too decrepit to fit in with the company's

master plan to create a new image for its postwar passenger service. The NP was not being uncommonly inventive; actually, the company had dragged its feet while the revolution in rolling stock was being fomented by the CB&Q and others. Manufacturers had learned much during the 1930s about weight-reducing design and materials while building the so-called streamliners. At long last, then, the NP's mechanical personnel were ready to jump on the bandwagon, too, even if the car builders were in no position to accommodate them with early delivery.

Late in 1944, well before the war had ended, the NP opted to go all out with a completely new, lightweight, streamlined *North Coast Limited*. The board of directors quickly approved an order for 36 passenger coaches. In the spring of 1945, six 5,400-horsepower diesel locomotives, 12 head-end cars, six dining cars, and 24 sleepers were added to the order. It was clear that the NP meant business.[4]

But first, several hurdles had to be cleared. Unfortunately, almost all other Class I railroads were badly in need of new cars; builders had to retrofit and expand to meet the unprecedented flood of requisitions; and the manufacture of even one new car required authorization by the War Production Board. This was because some of the materials needed for construction were still restricted. As a result, the NP's orders were backordered, and the new train could not make it into the timetable until 1947.

And that was when the dining car department discovered its miscalculation. In collaboration with the passenger department, Alec Thomson and Bill Paar had decided their new rolling restaurants should be designed to provide the most complete service ever offered on an NP diner. They were considerably more democratic than any previous cars had been: patrons could select "full-course meals in . . . [a] dining room section or a snack at the lunch counter."[5] This new departure occupied one end of the car and could accommodate eight persons. But to the dismay

Bill Paar, assistant superintendent of the dining car department, posed with famed polar explorer Roald Amundsen in April 1925, before Amundsen's first attempt to fly over the North Pole. Fred Kaul baked the cake.

of everyone involved, the snack bar was largely ignored by the passengers, who obviously wanted to avoid anything that smacked of economy or austerity. It seemed they wanted to put as much distance as possible between themselves and lingering memories of some 15 years of depression and wartime privations. One by one, then, the new cars were sent to the shop and remodeled to a standard dining car configuration: tables only, with seating for 48.

The NP's passenger revenues were at the threshold of the most stable period in their history. It was an almost eerie stability. Receipts were nearly $7.6 million in 1947, just over $7.6 million in 1966. They averaged $7.3 million annually from 1947 to 1956, $7.1 million from 1957 to 1966. However, the number of passengers declined steadily from 1.2 million in 1947 to 750,000 two decades later. Revenues stayed relatively even because, although patronage was dwindling, the distance traveled by each passenger rose. Average annual trip mileage during that period ranged from a low of 257 in 1949 to the highest ever at 558 in 1962, the year of Seattle's Century 21 Exposition. (The lowest average in modern times was 68 miles in 1915.) In 1952 the transcontinental *Mainstreeter* made its debut as the railroad's second streamliner. In what proved to be the last big push to increase passenger service, the schedule of the *North Coast Limited* was speeded up by 12 hours between Chicago and the North Pacific Coast, primarily by eliminating stops at many smaller cities. The new train was then installed on the former *North Coast Limited* schedule.

In general, NP trains were being used by confirmed rail travelers, repeaters who genuinely preferred them to cars, planes, or buses, and whose journeys took them farther from home each year. Oddly enough, they were neither more nor less inclined to patronize the dining cars than their predecessors were; in almost every year, the department's "production" average was three meals for every two passengers carried by the railroad. This was true in 1944, as well as in 1964.

But changes there were, despite the monotony of the statistical record. On October 1, 1948, Alec Thomson retired at the age of 70 after 54 years with the NP, 48 of them in the dining car department. He had headed the operation for 24 years, longer than any other superintendent, yet he did little to put his stamp on the department. True, his times were inimical to innovation: his career was marked by two wars that were separated by the worst economic depression this country ever suffered. In the end, perhaps, even though he introduced not a solitary house specialty, no one may deny him his place in NP dining car annals for the very good reason that he allowed nothing to detract from the company's reputation for "Famously Good" food, despite the odds against him.

His successor, Bill Paar, fared somewhat better. One morning in 1912, as the teen-aged Paar was delivering lunch to his railroading father, he chanced to walk by the commissary, then in the Mississippi Street Shops complex, at the very moment when Hazen Titus was leaving the building. The superintendent chatted with him for a few minutes, then quite suddenly offered the short, husky 14-year-old a job. He accepted on the spot and "never, ever regretted it." Paar would spend the next 56 years in the dining car service, working under six different superintendents, five of them during his first 12 years. None would have as much to do with his dining car philosophy as the first of them, his idol, Titus, the man whose contributions to Northern Pacific dining car service may be said to have survived the company itself.[6]

Bill Paar's innovations were small but numerous. None was the sort that would inspire an advertising campaign or transport an NP guest into gourmet heaven, but each had the virtue of adding immensely to the enjoyment of a meal without calling attention to itself. Such, for example, was his insistence that the chef alone be responsible for brewing the coffee, that he brew it as needed, but not less frequently than every half-hour, and that he dispose of the previous batch entirely, even if not a single cup of it had been poured.

He knew, too, that for a true coffee lover the first cup of the day was something special. Waiters were instructed that anyone who entered the car at breakfast was to be seated and immediately asked if he or she would like a pot of coffee. This was a departure from a rule that required stewards to make initial contact with all guests, but Paar knew the morning coffee ritual was entitled to a separate code of ceremonial form and courtesy.

Rules governed every aspect of dining car service, and in his book it was woe to any man who dared to breach one. Scarcely a day passed when he did not issue one of his legendary instruction forms. In these, coffee was an "all-important beverage" that had the power to leave "an everlasting impression" on the NP's guests, who were almost invariably described as "our valued patrons." He fired off one of these bulletins on October 17, 1960, after having observed a waiter place a "shelf-size" jar of mustard before an unsuspecting patron. It reveals as little else can the importance he attached to even the smallest courtesy:

SUBJECT: *Mustard Service.*

In no instance and under no circumstances should Waiter bring a full jar of mustard, French or otherwise, to the Dining Room table, and allow the guest to help himself from such a decided disadvantage.

Small, covered mustard pots are on all cars and, when mustard is desired by patron, Waiter should bring a small mustard pot containing about half-full quantity of mustard. Underline with a small demi-tasse saucer and provide a demi-tasse coffee spoon placed on the small plate to enable guests to use quantity of mustard desired.[7]

In preserving all that proved beneficial to the NP dining car service, in searching constantly for different ways to prepare foods, and in being ever alert to possible variations on older themes, Supt. Paar was but making certain he did not deviate from a course set and groomed by all those who

preceded him. It was little different from receiving an inheritance, enhancing it, then passing it on. For example, the NP whole wheat bread always had been popular, but Paar tried adding Roman Meal cereal—made by Roman Meal mills of Tacoma—to it and, thus, greatly improved it, in his estimation. And the owners of Lehmann Farms, of Lake Elmo, Minnesota, found him ready to try their pickled mushrooms on his relish trays.

Paar nurtured tradition with little gestures that loomed large in the public eye. During the Christmas season he presented slices of NP Fruit Cake to dining car patrons and holly corsages to every woman passenger on the *North Coast Limited*, all free of charge. In November, during National Apple Week, his guests enjoyed selected specimens of Delicious and Golden Delicious apples purchased from the Yakima Fruit Growers Association. This, also, was part of his continuing efforts to promote produce of the railway's territory on the dining cars. It was his way of helping get additional freight business for the company.

In these efforts he was aided by the advertising and publicity department, which was managed by L. L. Perrin, a former city editor for the *St. Paul Pioneer Press*. Perrin had joined the NP in 1927 as advertising assistant to the general passenger agent and was a capable and willing accomplice, ready to capitalize on any opportunity.

One Sunday evening in 1959, not long after the 50th anniversary of the Great Big Baked Potato, a western contestant appeared on "What's My Line?" the vastly popular, nationally syndicated, prime-time television game show. Among its regular panelists was Bennett Cerf, New York writer, editor, publisher, wit, and raconteur. When the guest had signed in on the blackboard, he wrote that his home was in Idaho. Instantly, Cerf beamed and said, "Every time I hear about Idaho I'm reminded of those great big potatoes they serve on the Northern Pacific Railroad's dining cars."

The next morning, Perrin called Paar and asked him to pick out about 20 pounds of the largest potatoes he could find in the commissary root cellar and send them to Cerf.

Canisters used for the NP's famous five-pound fruit cakes in 1955

At the same time, he penned a thank-you note, including the information that these huge tubers were grown in the Columbia Basin of Washington State, not in Idaho, despite that state's well-deserved reputation for growing fine baking potatoes. Fair is fair, he wrote, and suggested that Cerf could set the record straight by making a correction during the next week's edition of "What's My Line?"

A sincerely apologetic humorist addressed a gracious thank-you note in return and assured Perrin that he would never make the same mistake again. He said he would be certain to identify the source of the potatoes correctly if he

The Great Big Baked Potato neared its golden anniversary in 1957, when this photo was taken to publicize the new dining cars on the Vista-Dome *North Coast Limited*.

had occasion to mention them in the future, but that he really could not take up time on the show to correct his error. As a matter of fact, of course, the ad manager had not expected him to agree, and both he and Paar were pleased enough with the gratuitous publicity the railroad had gained in the first place.

As much as Paar enjoyed hearing compliments paid to established specialties, however, he knew total success lay in balancing the one with the changing tastes of the dining public. This last of the old-school dining car superintendents kept abreast of new developments in the food industry by voraciously reading books (especially cookbooks), magazines, newspapers, and newsletters and bulletins. He was on countless mailing lists to receive the latter, but he particularly welcomed those published by food councils, associations, and bureaus. Most often these were aimed at promoting wider use of their commodities or preparations, such as milk and dairy products, apples, eggs, beef, potatoes, and spices and seasonings. Both volumes of *The Gourmet Cookbook,* published in 1950 and 1957, as well as Gourmet Incorporated's *Bouquet de France: An Epicurean Tour of the French Provinces,* held honored places in his library. All were well-thumbed and bristling with place markers.[8]

Just as he freely accepted news and recipes from any reputable source, so was he most eager to share his with others. *Better Homes and Gardens* writers began requesting NP recipes in the 1930s and continued to do so well into the 1960s. Paar responded immediately to each inquiry. An executive of the Gerlach-Barlow Company, calendar publishers, saw a number of the company's dining car recipes in an American Car and Foundry Company pamphlet in 1949 and promptly asked for a similar collection to include in his popular recipe calendar for 1951. Paar complied by sending eight of them, including the ones for Puget Sound Clam Chowder, Canapé of Shrimp, Great Big Baked Potatoes, French Dressing, and, of course, the legendary NP Fruit Cake.[9]

But if Paar was the soul of kindness and generosity when dealing with people outside the company, his mode of sharing with those on the inside was susceptible to different interpretations. Many NP personnel who did not work with him or know him well regarded Paar as a latter-day Simon Legree, a tyrannical overseer cast from the same mold as countless despotic division superintendents of railroad legend. Contrariwise, his men saw him in an altogether different light. Leon Hampton, of St. Paul, a waiter from 1943 to 1980, knew him as "the easiest man in the world to work for, as long as you did your job. Bill Paar would bark, real loud," he explained, "but his bite was very small." As Leon told it, "We had some real nice men to work with—stewards, cooks *and* waiters. But the boss was something else." He was a soft-hearted person who went out of his way to counsel a family man not to worry, particularly after he had administered a severe reprimand.[10]

Others have noted that Paar was inordinately proud of never having discharged an employee. Drexel Pugh, who became a waiter in St. Paul the same year as Hampton, said this was true, that he might "put a man on the ground" (lay him off temporarily) but always called him back to work a few weeks later. This brief suspension without pay apparently was intended to give offenders time to consider a future with no regular pay check and missed opportunities for good tip income. Conveniently overlooked by both Paar and his supporters were those who were let go for cause—the few larcenous ones who brought everyone under suspicion and the alcoholics who could not or would not reform. Even these were given third and fourth chances before the superintendent could bring himself to remove them from service.

While some management experts might suggest his approach was doomed to fail, it had the opposite effect; apparently it brought his people much closer together. Most retired waiters cherish fond memories of that strong sense of family they enjoyed on the job; not just with each

OPPOSITE: Baker Joe Welligrant could bake 18 fruit cakes at once in the huge ovens of the St. Paul commissary, 1955.

other, but with all members of the crew, including the cooks and stewards, the commissary employees, the supervisors and the superintendent, who in most instances were white. Bob Jones, who became only the third black steward on the NP, said they got along well together because "we lived, slept, ate and worked together. Our quarters on the trains were in the dormitory car, where we even showered together. Our main objective was to take care of the passengers."

Drexel Pugh recalled how, at the end of their runs in Chicago and Seattle, Northern Pacific crews shared a cab to their hotel, while those of the Great Northern and other roads would split up and take separate transportation. "One would go this way, one that way," he said, "but everybody was going to the same place. It was pretty rough for those guys." One retired railroad waiter from St. Paul had begun his career at the NP but was laid off when business declined. Soon he found permanent employment with the GN, he said, but he never stopped trying to get back to his first employer because he missed the feeling "that we all were a family." In his opinion, blacks who gained seniority in the Northern Pacific's dining car service truly had the best of all possible worlds.

Bob Jones was quick to second the motion. He recalled how, even after having been promoted to steward, he enjoyed the respect and friendship of fellow employees and passengers alike. One incident stood out in his mind.

> You know, going west out of Seattle, the last night into Mandan and Bismarck, we'd be in St. Paul the next morning. I would have a farewell speech over the PA [public address] system that I would read to the passengers. Well, Dick Carlson, who ended up as assistant superintendent to Bud Bush after Paar retired, sat down with me and helped create some comments. Something like, "Tomorrow morning we'll be arriving in St. Paul. This car will be taken out of service, so you'll have a new crew, a fresh crew, and plenty of supplies. We enjoyed our trip with you; it was tremendous. We want to wish you all well and hope you have a pleasant journey, wherever you're going." Anyhow, the general passenger agent—his name was Charlie Sheffield—he came back and pumped my hand and said, "That's what we need." You see, the other stewards were not doing that, but I was always trying to find ways to satisfy our customers. The best way to do that was to talk with them.

Dick Carlson grew up in Mahtomedi, Minnesota, and went with the NP in 1955, after having served as a meat inspector with the U.S. Department of Agriculture in South St. Paul, the Upper Midwest's premier livestock market and former meat-packing center. His first job on the railroad was "pearl diving" (dishwashing), a chore variously assigned to the third or fourth cook on dining cars, depending on who occupied the bottom rung of the ladder. But he stayed with it, working his way upward, one step at a time—cook, supervisor, assistant superintendent of the department (1968). Memories of his years in the dining car department tumbled from his lips almost as echoes of the pronouncements voiced by many of the others: camaraderie, respect, loyalty. "We were a real family."

Yet he remembers Paar as "a regular Jekyll and Hyde" who, despite his diminutive size, had a talent for making grown men tremble when he called them on the carpet. "But you know Bill," he added. "He had a hard shell, but he also had a soft heart; he couldn't make anything stick or hold anything against anybody for very long.

"For some reason or other he seemed to like me," Carlson said. "I seldom called him 'Mr. Paar'; most of the time it was 'Boss.' In a way, it was letting him know I was not afraid of him. I think he liked that in his people. . . . I couldn't bring myself to call him Bill until after he retired."[11]

Genuine affection may have been the leavening that quickened the department and its members, making of the mix one of the most successful dining car operations in the land. And members is an apt descriptive for the personnel, too. It was as if each perceived himself as belonging to an exclusive club in which they enjoyed a special relationship with each other, as well as with the head man, who managed to instill those feelings, even if he was not entirely aware of the fact. Of course, it may well have been that this phenomenon grew out of the real family connections that existed in the service, both among the employees on the cars and in the commissary.

Joseph F. Welligrant, for example, a St. Paul native, entered the department in 1914, two years after Paar. He became a baker, having learned the art from Fred Kaul, whom he later succeeded. Eventually, Joe's son Donald J. climbed aboard as a cook ("He took me in hand and taught me how to cook. He was a master," said Carlson) and, in due time, Donald Jr. was added to the staff, following in his dad's tracks. Young Don is a Burlington Northern employee—not in dining car service, of course, because the company no longer operates passenger trains—so the family has been part of the NP clan, in a sense, for nearly three-quarters of a century.

Bill Paar retired in 1968. This true catering master's departure was an omen that foretold the demise of dining car service as it had been known for nearly 87 years at the NP. In 1970 the company merged with the Great Northern and the joint subsidiary of both, the CB&Q, to become the Burlington Northern. Thus the Northern Pacific's direct association with rail food service ended in 1970. In truth, that event marked the end of "the best in the West" for all time. The BN continued to offer meals on steel wheels, but the change was dramatic and traumatic, especially for those who had invested their lives in the business.

The End of the Dining Car Service

CHANGES WERE ACTUALLY TAKING PLACE before Bill Paar's retirement. And even before 1966, when Louis W. Menk, former president of the CB&Q, became president of the Northern Pacific, the nation's railroad leaders had reached the conclusion that, bottom lines aside, passenger service was a losing proposition; no longer could aging equipment function as a showcase, an advertising medium for a railroad's ability to operate as a modern, efficient, full-service transportation entity. Some freight customers were seeing themselves as subsidizers of an expensive drive to save an albatross that defied preservation.[1]

Whatever Lou Menk may have believed during his year at the throttle of the Burlington, at the NP he was soon a leading spokesman for the advocates of discontinuance. To these pragmatists the goal was clearly defined: passenger trains had to go if the railroad industry were to remain viable and competitive. And at NP, a program to seek elimination of unprofitable passenger trains was already showing signs of success before he loped into his new tenth-floor office in St. Paul. Earlier that year, regulatory bodies had approved the discontinuance of a branch line passenger operation in North Dakota; a short, main-line run in the same state; service between Spokane and Lewiston, Idaho; and service that had been in place between St. Paul and Duluth for nearly a century.

Of course, none of this had any effect on Paar's department, but another program to cut costs, which began as an experiment in the Far West, did bring changes. A buffet car featuring self-service and "excellent meals at low cost" was substituted in 1966 for the full-service dining car on NP trains between Seattle and Portland. Apparently the passengers liked it, for management decided to expand the service to the *Mainstreeter* the following year. For many cooks and waiters, the introduction of the buffet car meant the end of their careers.

Happily, traditional table d'hôte and à la carte service was retained on the *North Coast Limited* when the *Mainstreeter* diner was surrendered to fast-food service. But as

the oldest "name" train west of the Mississippi was about to complete the first year in what would have been its eighth decade of service, the merger intruded.

Change was unobtrusive at first, but only because there had been a minimum of planning for the menus that would be used on March 2, 1970, and the days that immediately followed. Yet, when the transition was made, it was most abrupt. Former Great Northern personnel had been placed in control of the operation, and they conducted it as they had in the past. The trackside NP commissary was closed and merged operations were headquartered in St. Paul on Third Street (later Kellogg Boulevard) between Rosabel and Broadway, in the 19th-century St. Paul, Minneapolis and Manitoba building. Diner crews, wearing their starched whites and pushing laden hand trucks, had to cross busy Third Street and trudge several more blocks to stock cars. Former NP crewmen, used to the convenience of merely stepping out a door to do the same thing, were somewhat chagrined by this turn of events.

But they chuckled over an attempt to eliminate one NP tradition that predated the GN's completion to the Pacific in 1893. From the beginning, stewards on Northern Pacific dining cars had been charged with the responsibility of taking a guest's order. On most other railroads, patrons were required to write out their own checks, a task often made difficult by a car's motion. Not long after the merger, a former GN steward seated a woman on the *North Coast Limited* diner and, as had been his custom for many years, dropped a check and pencil on the table before her. He could not know, of course, that she was Martha Jane Menk, wife of the new Burlington Northern president, the man who had been president of the NP before the merger. Mrs. Menk preferred the tried-and-true check-writing-by-the-steward method used on the former NP and reported this to her husband when she returned to St. Paul. John Garrity, Menk's executive assistant, sent a note to the new director of dining car service, informing him that only one person wrote food orders on that train. Subsequently,

TODAYS SPECIAL
FISH
CHOW MEIN
SWIS STEAK
HOT TURKEY SAND
ICE CREAM 20
MILK 20
JUICE 20
BREAD 10
LUNCH STARTS AT NOON
SOUP 30
HOT DOGS 35
HAMBURGER 65
CHILI 50

dining car stewards, at least on trains operated over lines of the former Northern Pacific, were instructed to perform that task for their guests, many of whom had never had to write their own before.

But if the cooks and waiters of NP lineage were uncomfortable with any changes thrust upon them by merger, they were aghast at what took place on May 1, 1971, even though they had been forewarned of the event. For that was the day Amtrak took on a nationwide schedule of intercity passenger trains.

Gone was the *North Coast Limited*, and the *Mainstreeter*, too. With them went the last vestiges of the first regular

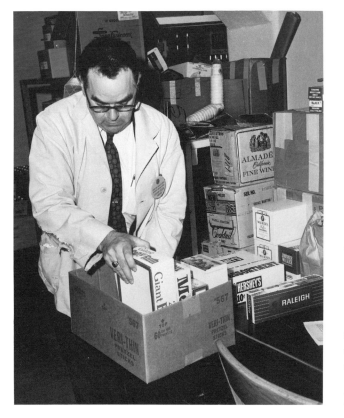

Glenn R. Johnstone, of White Bear Lake, Minnesota, packed candy bars, cigarettes, and small bottles of liquor for the buffet diner of the westbound *Mainstreeter* in 1968.

dining car service to the North Pacific Coast, or anywhere else on the shores of that ocean. Drexel Pugh was close to anger when he exclaimed, "That's when we became acquainted with paper—paper napkins, paper plates, paper cups! We didn't enjoy it, either," he added. "Because we weren't used to piling everything on one plate."

According to Leon Hampton, it was hard for waiters to adjust to the latter, especially in the beginning, because when they served an entire meal on a single plate, they did not feel they were "doing the job" they were used to doing. He noted, too, that it was very difficult for customers to accept, because they enjoyed the time-honored ritual of being served one course at a time and lingering over their coffee. "Matter of fact," he concludes, "we lost *all* service with Amtrak, the service we knew how to give."

Dick Carlson explained that Amtrak actually started out under near-normal conditions, having purchased cars, china, silver, and napery from the railroads. In 1980, when drastic budget cuts were mandated by the U.S. Congress, plastic tableware, paper napkins, prepackaged foods and microwave ovens made their debut on trains throughout the land, and rail dining became almost a carbon copy of airline meals. After passengers rebelled over food service, there was an almost complete reversal in 1984.

Today, silverware is back and, although the plates are still plastic, they are much heavier. Menus are standard across Amtrak's system, but chefs are urged to apply their art to enhance the meals they cook. Moreover, regional favorites, especially in seafoods, are served in every part of the country. Dining cars now seat 72, a 50 percent increase over the old limit of 48. This is possible because the cars are double-decked, and kitchens are on the lower level. They boast convection ovens and a grill, as well as a steam table. But as Bob Jones says, "No matter what they do, they'll never match the food and service we had on the old NP."

To which most confirmed rail travelers would add a heartfelt, "Amen!"

W riters and readers who love history are not as far apart in their desires and needs for documentation of facts in a book as each may believe. What can intrude, and usually does, is practicability. Providing the source for each and every statement of fact would exceed its bounds and burden many readers with trivia not germane to their interests. Yet all want to be assured that the book's foundations are sound.

This book's annotation aims at a middle ground. In many cases, sources are included within the body of the text. A large number of others are cited in the endnotes that follow. In general, specific documentation is provided for all direct quotes and specific figures cited; general sources are provided for background information.

Unpublished sources include letters and documents that are part of the records of the Northern Pacific Railway Company, located at the Minnesota Historical Society, St. Paul. In addition, records that were solicited by the author and collected by the late William F. Parr from former members of his staff; transcripts of interviews by the author with retired employees of the dining car department; and correspondence between Mr. Paar and the author while the latter was an employee of the Northern Pacific and Burlington Northern public relations department are all in the author's possession. Other sources include the following:

John Mickelsen scrapbooks 1-8, in the author's possession. They deal, for the most part, with NP history. Three others (one of which has disappeared) were devoted to biographical material. Mickelsen worked for the NP from 1898 to 1952. His interest in NP history was aroused after he became a draftsman in the engineering department. Eventually, he grew to be known as company historian, and his work was regarded as the ultimate source by NP officials.

Paul Rigdon Files, an unpublished history of the Union Pacific Railroad, held at the Union Pacific Historical Museum, Omaha. Rigdon was the museum's curator in the late 1940s and early 1950s (Ken Longe, UP research specialist, to the author, May 9, 1986). The files are not available to the public.

Some Personal Observations

1. Richard W. Luckin, *Dining on Rails: An Encyclopedia of Railroad China* (Denver: RK Publishing, 1983); John H. White, Jr., *The American Railroad Passenger Car*, 2 vols. (1 vol., 1978; Baltimore: Johns Hopkins University Press, 1985); Will C. Hollister, *Dinner in the Diner* (Los Angeles: Trans-Anglo Books, 1965).
2. Eric Partridge, *Origins: A Short Etymological Dictionary of Modern English* (New York: Macmillan Company, 1959, 1958).

1. A Trip in a Dining Car

1. NP, *Annual Report*, 1925, p. 12; interview of Robert J. Jones with author, December 17, 1985.
2. Interview of Jones with author, June 29, 1988.
3. Interviews of Jones with author, December 26, 1985, and June 29, 1988.
4. Jones interview, June 29, 1988.
5. Interview of Richard E. Carlson with author, June 29, 1988.
6. Jones interview, June 29, 1988.
7. Carlson interview, June 29, 1988.
8. "Purchases of over $300.00 Made by Dining Car Department—Months: of January, February and March, 1966."
9. *Time Table, Spring and Summer—Issued April 24, 1966*.
10. Transcript of audio-tape interview of Littleton Gardner with Anne R. Kaplan, St. Paul, May 10, 1988, in author's possession.
11. During 1929 seven second-class coaches were converted into combination baggage-dormitory cars for use on the *North Coast Limited*. These were NP's first dormitory cars for dining car crews. NP, *Annual Report*, 1929, p. 9.
12. *Time Table, Spring and Summer, 1966*.
13. Jones interview, June 29, 1988.
14. *Time Table, Spring and Summer, 1966*.

Notes

109

15. Jones interview, June 29, 1988.
16. Interview of William F. Paar with author, September 15, 1982.
17. Jones interview, December 17, 1985.
18. Gardner interview.
19. Here and in the following paragraph, see Northern Pacific Railway Company, *Guide to Points of Interest on the Scenic Route across America: Route of the Vista-Dome North Coast Limited* (St. Paul: The Company, 1966), 18, copy in MHS.
20. Jones interview, December 17, 1985.
21. Jones interviews, December 17, 1985, June 29, 1988.
22. Copy in author's possession.
23. Jones interview, June 29, 1988.

2. Eating on the Road

1. Gen. 42:27.
2. Geoffrey Chaucer, prologue to *Canterbury Tales*; *Encyclopaedia Britannica*, 14th ed. (1968 printing), s.v. "hotels and inns," "restaurants."
3. For more on diners on British railroads, see Neil Wooler, *Dinner in the Diner: The History of Railway Catering* (North Pomfret, Vt.: David and Charles, Inc., 1988).
4. White, *Passenger Car*, 3, 8, 12. The information on coach design and the beginnings of dining cars in the U.S., discussed in the rest of this chapter, is drawn from White, *Passenger Car*, chapter 4, and Paul Rigdon Files (hereafter Rigdon Files), 715-24, unpublished history of the Union Pacific Railroad, Union Pacific Museum, Omaha, Nebraska.
5. On Pullman's career, see White, *Passenger Car*, 246-57.
6. As quoted in Rigdon Files, 715-24.
7. Rigdon Files, 718.

3. Building the Northern Pacific

1. Matt. 19:30, 20:16; Mark 10:31; Luke 13:30. On Jefferson and the 1784, 1785, and 1787 Ordinances, here and in the following two paragraphs, see Howard R. Lamar, ed., *The Reader's Encyclopedia of the American West* (New York: Thomas Y. Crowell Company, 1977), s.v. "Jefferson, Thomas," "territorial system," and "Northwest Ordinance"; Benjamin H. Hibbard, *A History of the Public Land Policies*, Land Economics Series, ed. Richard T.

Ely (New York: Macmillan Company, 1924), 37-41, 82-86; Eugene V. Smalley, *History of the Northern Pacific Railroad* (New York: G. P. Putnam's Sons, 1883), 20-23 (quotations, 21).
2. *Memorial of Robert Mills, Submitting a New Plan of Roadway*, 29th Cong., 1st sess., 1846, H. Doc. 173 (Serial 485), 2; [Olin D. Wheeler,] "The Story of a Railway," in *Wonderland 1900* (St. Paul: Northern Pacific Railway Company, 1900), 77-79; Smalley, *History*, 51-56 (quotation, 52).
3. On Whitney, see Smalley, *History*, 57-68 (quotation, 58); Asa Whitney, *National Railroad Connecting the Atlantic and Pacific* ([Washington, D.C., 1845]); *Memorial of Asa Whitney, of New York City, Relative to the Construction of a Railroad from Lake Michigan to the Pacific Ocean*, 28th Cong., 2nd sess., 1845, H. Doc. 72 (Serial 464), 1-4. On Johnson, see Smalley, *History*, 69-76; "Early Northern Pacific History," *The Northwest* (St. Paul and Minneapolis), February 1885, p. 11; Edwin F. Johnson, *Railroad to the Pacific: Northern Route: Its Central Character, Relative Merits, etc.*, 2nd ed. (New York: Railroad Journal Job Printing Office, 1854). On Davis and the middle route, see Smalley, *History*, 89-96, 116; *Statutes at Large of the United States of America* 12 (Public Laws): 489-98.
4. Smalley, *History*, 106-10, 116-17.
5. Smalley, *History*, 161-62, 166-67.
6. C[harles] E. Denney, *The Northern Pacific: First of the Northern Transcontinentals* (New York: Newcomen Society in North America, 1949). This address, delivered by NP's president before the society on May 18, 1949, was written by L. L. Perrin, the railway's advertising manager and a former city editor for the *St. Paul Pioneer Press*.
7. Here and in the following two paragraphs, see Smalley, *History*, 185-87; "Early Northern Pacific History," *The Northwest*, April 1885, p. 2, 3; Carl Zapffe, *Brainerd, Minnesota, 1871-1946: Seventy-fifth Anniversary* (Brainerd: Brainerd Civic Association, 1946), 3-5; "The Northwest on Wheels!" *The Northwest*, June 1885, p. 2-5.
8. Elizabeth B. Custer, *"Boots and Saddles": Or, Life in Dakota with General Custer* (New York: Harper & Brothers, 1885), 95-96 (quotation). This last paragraph—and a misreading of dates—gave rise to an erroneous boast by Will Hollister that the company had operated a primitive dining car service in 1876 (*Dinner in the Diner*, 93). The lunchroom stand-ins, spotted on house tracks near NP depot buildings, were not, in fact, employed in train service.

9. "The Northwest on Wheels!" *The Northwest*, July 1885, p. 5.

10. Mickelsen scrapbook, 2:120 (quotation); U.S., Geological Survey, *Guidebook of the Western United States: The Northern Pacific Route*, Bulletin 611 (Washington, D.C.: Government Printing Office, 1915), 51. On the Sioux and their relations with the railroad, see John W. Bailey, *Pacifying the Plains: General Alfred Terry and the Decline of the Sioux, 1866-1890* (Westport, Conn.: Greenwood Press, 1979), 70, 80-87.

11. Here and in the following paragraph, see Smalley, *History*, 198-203, 206-10, 213-17.

12. Custer, *"Boots and Saddles,"* 253-54; NP, *Annual Report*, 1876, p. 15. Colonel Clement A. Lounsberry, owner of the *Bismarck Tribune*, was a passenger on this train. He later recalled that the snowplow was at first connected to the train, moving it in fits and starts, but that the plow was sent ahead after Custer complained; as the train's conductor had predicted, a huge drift formed between the train and the plow before they could be reconnected. The train was stranded for 16 days, and the company had a $15,000 deficit for the month, highest among three months that fiscal year in which NP reported negative net income. "A Story of 1876: Snow-Bucking and Other Incidents—Reminiscences of the Opening of the Black Hills," *The Record: Historical, Personal and Other Sketches* (Fargo, N.Dak.), January 1897, p. 2-5; Mickelsen scrapbook 1:203; NP, *Annual Report*, 1876, p. 38.

13. On passenger equipment and income, here and below, see minutes from meetings of the board of directors, March 22, September 14, November 16, 1871, and December 17, 1879, in vol. 3, p. 140, 232, 233, and vol. 5, p. 120—all in Secretary, Minutes and Related Records, 1864-1956, Northern Pacific Railway Company, St. Paul, Records, Minnesota Historical Society (hereafter NP Records, MHS); NP, *Annual Report*, 1880, p. 6. Reference to "wild scheme" quoted in Smalley, *History*, 204.

14. Here and in the following paragraph, see NP, *Annual Report*, 1880, p. 16, 8 (quotations, 8).

15. A. P. Farrar to H. E. Sargent, April 8, 1881, Letters Received: 1877-84 (April) series, General Manager dept., NP Records, MHS.

16. A. P. Farrar to H. Haupt, May 24, 1881, Letters Received: 1877-84 (April) series, General Manager dept., NP Records, MHS. The author learned of Hill's land purchase in the late 1970s while working in the NP's records of land patents, sales, and deeds, now in the BN's Seattle offices. Hill's son-in-law,

George Slade, later purchased 3,000 acres near Dawson, North Dakota, for a hunting club; it is now Slade National Wildlife Refuge. *Dawson Centennial, 1880-1980: Dawson, North Dakota, the First 100 Years* ([Dawson?, N.Dak.: n.p., 1980]), 15-20.

4. Henry Villard and the NP Dining Car Service

1. On Villard, here and in the next five paragraphs, see Smalley, *History*, 245-66; Robert S. Macfarlane, *Henry Villard and the Northern Pacific* (New York: Newcomen Society in North America, 1954). The latter, an address written by L. L. Perrin, was delivered before the society in New York on January 27, 1954. It underwent two printings to satisfy the demand for copies from historians and students of business history. See also Henry Villard, *Memoirs of Henry Villard, Journalist and Financier, 1835-1900*, 2 vols. (Boston and New York: Houghton, Mifflin and Company, 1904), especially 2:270-316.

2. Here and in the following paragraph, see Smalley, *History*, 265-70; Macfarlane, *Villard*, 16 (quotation).

3. The *Annual Report* for 1881 shows 1,065 miles of line operated, but this includes 75.5 miles between St. Paul and Sauk Rapids that were leased from predecessors of the Great Northern.

4. NP, *Annual Report*, 1879, 1880, 1881.

5. NP, *Annual Report*, 1882, 1883. The average number of track miles operated increased by 36 percent, while passenger income increased by 92 percent and passenger miles traveled by 125 percent.

6. T. F. Oakes to Gen. H. Haupt, November 14, 1882, Letters Received: 1877-84 (April) series, General Manager dept., NP Records, MHS.

7. Here and in the following paragraph, see G. W. Cross to H. Haupt, November 30, 1882 (quotation), Letters Received: 1877-84 (April) series, General Manager dept., NP Records, MHS.

8. Here and in the following paragraph, see L. G. Matthews to Henry Villard, November 22, 1882, and T. F. Oakes to Geo. M. Pullman, November 3, 1882 (quotation), both copies in letterpress book, Letters Sent: 1875-1919 series, Vice President subgroup, President dept., NP Records, MHS.

9. Author's notes from clippings in Pullman company scrapbooks, The Newberry Library, Chicago.

10. G[.] W[.] Cushing to T. F. Oakes, January 23, 1883 (quotation), Letters Received: Registered, President and Vice President: 1882-93 series, President dept., NP Records, MHS.

11. Reprinted in *The Northwest* (New York), April 1883, p. 12.

12. Pullman, Illinois, was Pullman's factory town outside Chicago. Geo. M. Pullman to T. F. Oakes, April 7, 1883 (quotation), Letters Received: Registered, President and Vice President: 1882-93 series, President dept.; G. W. Cushing to James B. Williams, September 21, 1883, Special Papers no. 68, Special Papers, Registered: President and Vice President: 1882-96 series, President dept.—both in NP Records, MHS.

13. Here and in the following two paragraphs, see Cushing to Williams, September 21, 1883; James B. Williams to H. D. Bulkley, January 8, 1884, Special Papers no. 68, Special Papers, Registered: President and Vice President: 1882-96 series, President dept.—both in NP Records, MHS.

14. Author's notes from clippings in Pullman company scrapbooks, Newberry Library.

15. Author's notes from clippings in Pullman company scrapbooks, Newberry Library.

16. Cha[rles] L. Fleming to J[oseph] M. Graham, May 7, 1883 (quotation), Henry A. Libby to E. J. Westlake, May 5, 1883, Westlake to J. T. Odell, May 9, 1883, Odell to H. Haupt, May 14, 1883 (quotation)—all in Letters Received: 1877-84 (April) series, General Manager dept., NP Records, MHS.

17. Cushing to Williams, September 21, 1883.

18. Author's notes from clipping in Pullman company scrapbooks, Newberry Library.

19. Author's notes from *Inter-Ocean* clippings in Pullman company scrapbooks, Newberry Library; "The Chicago Exposition of Railway Appliances," Editorial Correspondence sec., *Railroad Gazette* (New York), July 27, 1883, p. 409-501 (quotation, 500).

20. Sup[erintendent of] Mach[inery] [A. P. Farrar] to H. Haupt, August 31, 1881, Letters Received: 1877-84 (April) series, General Manager dept., NP Records, MHS.

21. G. W. Cross to H. Haupt, January 13, 1882, Letters Received: 1877-84 (April) series, General Manager dept., NP Records, MHS.

22. G. W. Cushing to H. Haupt, November 27, 1882, Letters Received: 1877-84 (April) series, General Manager dept., NP Records, MHS.

23. "Pullman Palace Car Co., Bills for 17 Emigrant Sleepers & 10 Dining Cars," ledger pages, October 3, 1883, Special Papers no. 68, Special Papers, Registered: President and Vice President: 1882-96 series, President dept., NP Records, MHS. The *Inter-Ocean* article is quoted above.

24. Geo. M. Pullman to T. F. Oakes, January 26, 1883, Letters Received: Registered, President and Vice President: 1882-93 series, President dept., NP Records, MHS.

25. James B. Williams to H. D. Bulkley, January 8, 1884, and "Dining Car., Nor[.] Pac[.]," ledger pages, about April 1883, both in Special Papers no. 68, Special Papers, Registered: President and Vice President: 1882-96 series; G. W. Cushing to T. F. Oakes, January 23, 1883 (quotation), Letters Received: Registered, President and Vice President: 1882-93 series—all in President dept., NP Records, MHS.

5. Transcontinental Service and Financial Upheaval

1. Here and in the following five paragraphs, see Smalley, *History*, 290-92; NP, *Annual Report*, 1881, p. 35; E. V. S[malley], "The Northern Pacific Opening," *The Northwest* (New York), October 1883, p. 9, 10. The spike was the first one used on the NP at Thomson Junction in 1870. Company tradition held that it had been preserved by H. C. Davis, who "struck the first blow" in 1870 as an NP employee. In 1883 he was working for James J. Hill's St. Paul, Minneapolis and Manitoba, and he attended the ceremonies as a special guest.

2. When Mohr returned to Bremen in November, he collected the articles and, with some additions and revisions, published them in book form as *Ein Streifzug durch den Nordwesten Amerikas: Festfahrt zur Northern Pacific-Bahn im Herbste 1883* (Berlin: Verlag von Robert Oppenheim, 1884). The book was published in English as *Excursion through America*, ed. Ray Allen Billington, translated by LaVern J. Rippley with the collaboration of Klaus Lanzinger (The Lakeside Classics, no. 71; Chicago: R. R. Donnelley & Sons Co., 1973) (quotations, 183-84, 233-34).

3. S[malley], "The Northern Pacific Opening," *The Northwest*, October 1883, p. 10. One of Smalley's tasks was to write a history of the company and publish it in time to present copies to all the guests. He managed the job, while establishing and editing *The Northwest*. This monthly journal was underwritten by Villard; in fact, Smalley's first office was in the Mills Building in New York, where the NP and its president maintained the company's executive offices.

4. Here and in the following paragraph, see *The Northwest*, April 1883, p. 23, August 1883, p. 27.

5. "Northern Pacific Policy," *The Northwest*, August 1883, p. 11. Muir's statement was reprinted from an article of June 28, 1883, in the *Portland Oregonian*.

6. Paar, personal files.

7. Here and in the following paragraph, see Villard, *Memoirs* 2:307-16 (quotations, 307, 308); "Mr. Villard's Resignation," *The Northwest*, January 1884, p. 9.

8. Personal Items sec., *The Northwest*, November 1883, p. 9.

9. NP, *Annual Report*, 1890, p. 31, 34, 82.

10. Here and in the following four paragraphs, see NP, *Annual Reports*, 1883-91.

6. Hazen Titus and the Great Big Baked Potato

1. Frank S. Farrell to Ralph W. Miller, associate editor, Standard Education Society, Inc., publishers, *New Standard Encyclopedia*, February 8, 1963, file copy in author's possession.

2. Here and in the following paragraph, see "The 'North Coast Limited,'" in *Wonderland 1901*, by Olin D. Wheeler (St. Paul: Northern Pacific Railway Company, 1901), 21; NP, *Annual Report*, 1900, p. 30. *Wonderland* was a promotional booklet published by Fee's office and copyrighted in his name.

3. Titus was well versed in the tribulations of the French agronomist Antoine-Auguste Parmentier who, a century earlier, had popularized the potato in France, where it had been scorned even more than the giants of Washington State. French farmers and housewives had regarded it as fodder and nothing more, until the persistent Parmentier convinced them of its worth as a tasty and nutritious vegetable. So well did he do his job that the tuber is still known as a Parmentier in some parts of the country, while elsewhere in France the name refers to mashed potatoes. Information here and in the following four paragraphs is from an interview of William F. Paar, about September 1957.

4. NP, *Northern Pacific Train Service*, 1909, pamphlet in collection of John E. Foote, Billings, Montana.

5. For figures, here and in the following two paragraphs, see annual reports. The NP changed from a January-December fiscal year to a July-June fiscal year in 1917.

6. NP, *On the Wings of the Wind*, 1911, pamphlet, Foote collection.

7. Records on the hotels were evidently destroyed when they no longer provided information necessary for current operations. Many lunchrooms remained under NP (later BN) operation until 1971.

8. NP, *Annual Report*, 1917, p. 16-17.

9. P. Harvey Middleton, *Railways and Public Opinion: Eleven Decades* (Chicago: Railway Business Association, 1941), 143.

10. Author's interview with William F. Paar, September 1, 1982, materials in possession of author.

11. S. A. Wilder to A. M. Burt, February 9, 1925, carbon, General Manager [Clifford L. Nichols] to J[oseph] H. Dyer, October 12, 1922, carbon (quotation)—both in U.S. Railroad Labor Board Files: 1920-57 series, Railway Mediation and Arbitration Boards subgroup, Chief of Labor Relations dept., NP Records, MHS.

12. Undated comparison of wages for various classes of dining car employees and numbers employed in each position, December 1915, 1917, et al.

7. Waiters and Unions

1. NP, *Annual Report*, 1921, p. 13, 1922, p. 15.

2. Fowler to Thompson, September 4, 1924, U.S. Railroad Labor Board Files: 1920-57 series, Railway Mediation and Arbitration Boards subgroup, Chief of Labor Relations dept., NP Records, MHS.

3. Fowler to Rapelje, December 11, 1924, Wilder to Rapelje, December 16, 1924, carbon, Thomson to Wilder, January 16, 1925, carbon—all in U.S. Railroad Labor Board Files: 1920-57 series, Railway Mediation and Arbitration Boards subgroup, Chief of Labor Relations dept., NP Records, MHS. Thomson referred to the workers as "boys," which is the only use of a possibly racist term by any member of NP management in all the correspondence examined while this book was being written. The same cannot be said for officers of other railroads with whom NP officials carried on an extensive correspondence during times of organizing efforts and contract negotiations. The word was, in fact, comparable to traditional railroad usage of terms such as "boys," "men," "gang," "crew," and thus probably bore no demeaning connotation.

4. Here and in the following paragraph, see Donnelly to Fowler, February 12, 1926, Letters Sent, 1919-70 series, President dept., NP Records, MHS; Wilder to Burt, February 9, 1925 (see chapter 6, note 11).

5. Burt to Fowler, February 14, 1925, U.S. Railroad Labor Board Files, Railway Mediation and Arbitration Boards subgroup, Chief of Labor Relations dept., NP Records, MHS.

6. Decision No. 3971, Docket 4840, Chicago, November 27, 1925, Brotherhood of Sleeping and Dining Car Employees' Union v. Northern Pacific Railway Co., in U.S. Railroad Labor Board, *Decisions of the United States Railroad Labor Board . . . 1925*

(Washington, D.C.: Government Printing Office, 1926), 1313-14.

7. Butler, Oliver, and Maxwell to Wilder, July 24, 1925 (quotation), Wilder to Thomson, July 28, 1925, carbon, "Memorandum of conference at 10:00 A.M., December 21st, [1925,] in the office of the Superintendent of the Dining Car Department," carbon (quotation)—all in U.S. Railroad Labor Board Files, Railway Mediation and Arbitration Boards subgroup, Chief of Labor Relations dept., NP Records, MHS.

8. "Minutes of meeting with Dining Car Waiters held in Mr. Thomson's Office[,] March 6, 1926," carbon, U.S. Railroad Labor Board Files: 1920-57 series, Railway Mediation and Arbitration Boards subgroup, Chief of Labor Relations dept., NP Records, MHS.

9. "Minutes of meeting held on May 10th, [1926,] to consider proposed constitution of the Association of Dining Car Waiters," carbon, "Draft, Constitution of the Association of Dining Car Waiters—Northern Pacific Railway Company," carbon—both in U.S. Railroad Labor Board Files: 1920-57 Series, Railway Mediation and Arbitration Boards subgroup, Chief of Labor Relations dept., NP Records, MHS.

10. "Draft, Constitution of the Association of Dining Car Waiters," U.S. Railroad Labor Board Files: 1920-57 series, Railway Mediation and Arbitration Boards subgroup, Chief of Labor Relations dept., NP Records, MHS.

11. On the 1936-37 negotiations, see correspondence in File 37, Non-Operating Employees Negotiating Files, Chief of Labor Relations dept., NP Records, MHS.

12. Paar interview, September 1, 1982; NP, *Annual Report,* 1955, p. 8.

13. NP, *Annual Report,* 1933, p. 6.

14. Interview of Paar with author, about May 1963.

8. Dining Car Line to the Pacific

1. The discussion here and in the following six paragraphs is based on Paar interview, 1963; interview of Robert C. Jones with author, December 17, 1985.

2. Jones interview, December 26, 1985.

3. Paar interview, September 15, 1982.

4. NP, *Annual Report,* 1944, p. 8, 1945, p. 8.

5. NP, *Annual Report,* 1947, p. 5.

6. Paar interview, September 15, 1982.

7. Paar, "*SUBJECT: Coffee Brewing.,*" bulletin, June 22, 1962, "*SUBJECT: Manners.,*" notice, June 14, 1963, "*SUBJECT: Mustard Service.,*" bulletin, October 17, 1960—all copies in possession of author.

8. Gourmet, *The Gourmet Cookbook,* 2 vols. (New York: Gourmet, 1950-57); Samuel Chamberlain, *Bouquet de France: An Epicurean Tour of the French Provinces* (New York: Gourmet, 1952).

9. Interview of Paar with author, December 1, 1982.

10. The discussion here and in the following four paragraphs is based on interviews of Leon Hampton and Drexel Pugh with author, December 18, 1985; Jones interview, December 26, 1985.

11. Carlson interview with author, January 22, 1986.

9. The End of the Dining Car Service

1. Information in this chapter is based on Carlson interview, January 22, 1986; Pugh interview; Hampton interview; and Jones interview, December 26, 1985.

The Recipes | 10

Beverages

Despite widespread bootlegging and smuggling, most Americans writhed beneath the yoke of the Volstead Act for 15 parched years. With ratification of the 21st Amendment on December 5, 1933, the railroads moved as quickly as possible to slake the thirsts of their passengers. When liquor was available once more, the NP's dining car department reacted typically, and on January 29, 1934, Supt. Thomson issued the first instruction sheet since World War I. Many of the stewards and waiters had joined the department during Prohibition, so the instruction sheet was rather more detailed than its predecessors. That sheet, entitled "Service Instructions Covering Wines, Liquors, and Mixed Drinks," is reprinted here.

NOTE: None of these recipes has been tested.

Scotch, Bourbon, and Rye Whiskeys

Serve in decanter 1 $\frac{1}{2}$ ounces to order. Serve whiskey glass and ale glass with ice water. Let guest pour own drink from decanter.

Gin

Serve in individual bottle with whiskey glass and ale glass of ice water.

Martini Cocktail

2 ounces gin
1 ounce Italian vermouth
1 dash Angostura bitters

Place 2 pieces ice in bar tumbler, add gin, vermouth, and bitters. Stir well and strain into stem cocktail glass. Place olive in glass with wood toothpick stuck in it.

Manhattan Cocktail

1 $\frac{1}{2}$ ounces rye whiskey
1 ounce Italian vermouth

Stir well in bar tumbler with ice and strain into stem cocktail glass with maraschino cherry. Stick a wood toothpick in cherry.

Old Fashioned Cocktail

1 lump sugar
1 $\frac{1}{2}$ ounces rye whiskey
1 dash Angostura bitters

Crush sugar and bitters together in bar tumbler; add [whiskey and] 2 or 3 pieces of ice. Stir well, garnish with $\frac{1}{2}$ slice of orange and a twist of lemon peel. Serve in the mixing glass without straining.

Orange Blossom Cocktail

1 $\frac{1}{2}$ ounces orange juice
2 ounces gin
$\frac{1}{2}$ ounce vermouth

Shake well with ice, strain into stem cocktail glass and serve.

Tom Collins

> *juice of ¹/₂ lemon*
> *2 ounces gin*
> *¹/₂ tablespoon sugar*
> *carbonated water or White Rock*

Stir lemon juice, gin, ice and sugar well in iced tea glass. Fill with charged water.

Silver Fizz

> *juice of ¹/₂ lemon*
> *¹/₂ tablespoon powdered sugar*
> *white of 1 egg*
> *2 ounces gin*

Shake well with ice, strain into iced tea glass, fill with charged water.

Golden Fizz

Same as above, but use yolk of egg in place of white.

Gin Fizz

Same as above, without egg.

Rickies

Use 8-ounce ale glass.

> *1 lump of ice*
> *juice of ¹/₂ lemon*

Add 1 ¹/₂ ounces Scotch, bourbon, gin or rye as wanted, fill with charged water.

Crème de Menthe

Fill cocktail stem glass with finely crushed ice. Pour crème de menthe over ice and serve with 2 short straws.

White Wines

Serve chilled but not iced. Serve in stem wine glass.

Red Wines

Remove from cooler when ordered and let remain on table until served. This should not be served cold. Serve in stem wine glass. Wine bottles should be stored in refrigerators on their sides so corks will remain wet. Do not shake bottles any more than necessary when serving and always pour wine to side of glass slowly.

Care of Glasses

See that all glasses are handled carefully and stored in buffet in such a manner as to avoid breaking. Do not wash them in the sink with other glassware. Remove them from the tables and wash in clean water and polish. The conductor will mix all drinks and pay particular attention to the serving of them.

Highballs

Serve the liquor in decanter, ale glass with ice, and the ginger ale or water in the bottle. Let guests mix own drinks at table. Observation Car porters can use the carbonated water from the fountain for rickies, fizzes, etc., where charged water is specified.

Wines

A supply of wines will be carried in dining cars only on Trains 1 and 2 and if Observation Car porter has a call for same he may get them from the dining car conductor and pay for them.

Breakfast Dishes

Rice and Ham Griddle Cakes

Very tender and tasty. The batter is thin.

>   2 eggs
>   1 cup cooked rice
>   2 cups milk
>   3 tablespoons melted butter
>   1 cup all-purpose flour
>   5 teaspoons baking powder
>   ¹/₂ teaspoon salt
>   1 cup cooked ham, diced

In medium bowl, beat eggs; add cooked rice, milk, and butter. Mix well.

Sift together flour, baking powder, and salt; add to above mixture; beat until well blended. Stir in diced ham.

Spoon batter onto a hot, greased griddle to form cakes of desired size. Cook on one side until a number of bubbles appear. Turn over and cook to a golden brown.

Serve hot with butter and syrup. Makes 15 griddle cakes, 4 inches in diameter.

German Pancake

Looks and tastes delicious.

>   3 eggs
>   ¹/₂ teaspoon salt
>   ¹/₂ cup all-purpose flour
>   ¹/₂ cup milk
>   2 tablespoons soft butter

In medium bowl, beat eggs until very light with rotary beater. Add salt and flour, then milk, beating all the time.

Spread soft butter on bottom and sides of a cold 10-inch frying pan. Pour in egg batter.

Bake 20 to 25 minutes in oven preheated to 400 degrees, gradually reducing heat to 325 degrees. The pancake should puff up at the sides and be crisp and brown.

Place on hot platter; serve with powdered sugar and lemon juice. Makes 2 servings.

French Toast

>   2 eggs, slightly beaten
>   ¹/₂ cup milk
>   1 tablespoon sugar
>   ¹/₄ teaspoon salt
>   ¹/₄ teaspoon cinnamon
>   butter or shortening

Cut 1 ½-inch slices of Toast Bread (see receipe p. 145) in half, diagonally.

Mix eggs, milk, sugar, salt, and cinnamon in a shallow dish. Dip bread into mixture; fry it in a little butter or shortening until golden brown on both sides. Serve hot with topping of your choice. Makes 3 slices.

German Potato Pancakes

Peel a large baking potato, then grate it.

Stir in 1 beaten egg; season with salt. A pinch at a time, add just enough flour to bind. Mix well (liquid from egg and potato should be sufficient moisture).

Make cakes thin and fry in hot oil until brown and tender. Makes 8 pancakes.

NOTE: The baking potatoes used in the dining cars were very large.

Washington Apple Pan Cake

3 eggs
2 tablespoons melted butter
¼ cup all-purpose flour
¼ cup cornstarch
1 teaspoon sugar
¹/₁₆ teaspoon salt
 dash of ground nutmeg (or more, to taste)
1 small apple, peeled and thinly sliced

Beat eggs in medium bowl. Add butter. Stir dry ingredients together; add to egg and butter mixture all at once.

Heat 2 well-buttered omelet pans over medium heat and pour half of batter in each. Sprinkle half of sliced apple over batter in each pan. Cook until partially set; fold the cakes in half; continue cooking until done.

Slide cakes onto warm plate. Sprinkle with powdered sugar; serve with slice of lemon. Makes 1 serving.

Omelet Cherbourg

3 tablespoons butter
3 tablespoons all-purpose flour
1 cup milk
 salt
 white pepper
½ cup frozen cooked shrimp, thawed
6 eggs
2 tablespoons water
 hot shrimp for garnish

In small saucepan, melt butter. Over medium heat, add flour; cook 1 minute. Add milk all at once, stirring well. Season with salt and white pepper, to taste. Cook until thick, stirring constantly. Add shrimp and heat 1 more minute; keep warm.

In small bowl, beat eggs and water just until well mixed. Season with salt and white pepper.

Pour egg mixture into 2 well-buttered omelet pans. Cook over medium heat until partially set. Place ⅓ of creamed shrimp mixture in center of each omelet; fold; cook until done.

Slide each omelet onto a warm plate. Pour remaining sauce around the omelets. Place a few hot shrimp on top of each omelet for garnish. Makes 2 servings.

Sweet Dough

One of these small, rich rolls was served on a bread plate with the toast for breakfast.

   3 *packages active dry yeast*
   2 *cups warm milk*
   $2/3$ *cup shortening*
  2 $1/4$ *cups sugar, divided*
   1 *tablespoon salt*
  $1/16$ *teaspoon ground mace*
   6 *eggs*
  $1/2$ *teaspoon vanilla extract*
10 $1/2$ *to 11 cups sifted all-purpose flour*
   4 *tablespoons melted butter*
   2 *teaspoons ground cinnamon*

Combine yeast with milk; let stand.

In large bowl, lightly cream shortening, 2 cups sugar, salt, and mace. Add eggs, one at a time, creaming well after each addition. Slowly add yeast and milk; add vanilla.

Beat in 3 cups flour. Add 3 more cups flour, one at a time, beating well with electric mixer after each addition. Using wooden spoon, gradually work in remaining flour, mixing until dough is stiff enough to leave sides of bowl.

Knead dough until smooth and elastic. Place in a greased bowl, turning to grease top. Cover and let rise until doubled, about 45 minutes.

Punch down dough; divide in half; let rest 10 minutes. Roll half of dough into a 12-by-16-inch rectangle. Brush with 2 tablespoons melted butter; sprinkle with 2 table-spoons sugar and 1 teaspooon cinnamon. Roll up from long side, jelly-roll fashion; pinch seam to seal. Cut crosswise into 15 slices and place slices in greased 9-by-13-inch pan, cut side down. Prepare other half in the same manner. Cover and let rise until doubled, about 40 minutes.

Bake at 375 degrees for 20 minutes. While still warm, frost with icing made from confectioners' sugar. Makes about 2 $1/2$ dozen 3-inch rolls.

Soups

Basic Stock

   veal bones, or beef bones with trimmings, or ham jell with scraps
12 *cups water*
 1 *clove garlic*
 4 *whole allspice*
 4 *whole white cloves*
 $1/2$ *teaspoon ground mace*
 1 *bay leaf*
   tops from one stalk celery

Place veal, beef, or ham in large kettle; cover with water. Add remaining ingredients. Bring to a hard, fast boil, then simmer for 3 to 4 hours. Strain. Use or refriger-ate immediately. Makes 2 quarts.

Minestrone Milanese

A large recipe. Divide and freeze.

¹/₄ pound ham, finely diced
¹/₄ pound fresh pork, finely diced
4 tablespoons butter
1 ¹/₂ cups minced onions
1 cup minced green onions and tops
1 ¹/₂ cups minced carrots
1 ¹/₂ cups minced celery
1 ¹/₂ cups diced turnips
1 ¹/₂ cups shredded cabbage
1 clove garlic
2 teaspoons salt
4 quarts beef stock
3 cups diced potatoes
2 cups crushed tomatoes
¹/₄ bunch parsley
1 cup peas
1 cup diced green beans
¹/₄ cup rice
¹/₂ teaspoon pepper

In 8-quart kettle, sauté ham and pork in butter; add onions, carrots, celery, turnips, and cabbage. Sauté all lightly. Do not brown.

Chop garlic with the salt until very fine and add to above mixture. Then add beef stock, remaining vegetables, and rice. Add pepper; adjust seasoning, if necessary. Cook approximately 2 hours, stirring occasionally. Makes 7 quarts.

Chicken Mulligatawny

1 small onion, diced
3 tablespoons butter
¹/₄ chicken, cooked and diced
1 teaspoon curry powder
3 tablespoons all-purpose flour
4 cups chicken stock
¹/₃ cup long grain rice
1 large green apple, peeled and diced

In medium fry pan, sauté onion in 2 tablespoons butter. Stir in chicken. Add curry powder; add flour, 1 tablespoon at a time; blend well.

Pour chicken stock into medium saucepan; add rice and sautéed chicken. Simmer, covered, for 30 minutes, stirring occasionally.

In fry pan, cook apple in remaining tablespoon butter until tender. Add to soup and simmer 10 minutes. Makes 1 ¹/₂ quarts.

Chicken Soup, Florentine

3 cups chicken broth
¹/₄ cup rice
¹/₂ cup cooked chicken, diced
1 cup milk
6 tablespoons all-purpose flour
6 tablespoons water
salt
pepper
chopped parsley

Pour chicken broth into large saucepan. Add rice; bring to a boil, reduce heat, and cook for 15 minutes. Add diced chicken and milk.

Continued on p. 122

Place flour in small bowl. Add 4 tablespoons water all at once. Stir with large spoon using back of spoon to work out any lumps. Add the remaining water 1 tablespoon at a time. Use this white sauce to thicken soup. Season with salt and pepper to taste. Garnish with chopped parsley. Makes 4 servings.

Old-fashioned Navy Bean Soup

  2 cups navy beans
    cold water to cover
  2 quarts stock, divided
    ham bone, trimmed of all skin
  1 medium onion, finely chopped
  1 stalk celery, chopped
  1 bay leaf
  6 whole black peppercorns
  2 parsley sprigs
  2 small carrots, finely diced
    salt
    pepper
  $1/16$ teaspoon ground nutmeg
  $1/2$ to 1 cup lean, boiled ham, finely chopped

Wash beans; cover with cold water and let stand overnight. Next morning discard water.

In soup kettle, place beans, 6 cups of stock, ham bone, and onion. Bring to boil, lower heat, and cook until beans are almost tender (a number of the beans will be cooked to pieces which will give the soup a thickened consistency).

In another pan, place celery, bay leaf, peppercorns, parsley, and 2 cups stock; boil 45 minutes; strain this stock into the beans.

Add carrots to beans; cook until carrots are tender, about 30 minutes.

Remove ham bone. Season with salt and pepper to taste; add nutmeg; add boiled ham. Simmer 10 minutes. When served, each portion should contain a reasonable amount of whole beans, carrots, and ham. Makes 6 servings.

NOTE: Water may be substituted for stock.

Oxtail Soup with Barley

  1 oxtail
    water
  $1/4$ cup butter
  1 medium onion, finely chopped
  1 small clove garlic
  4 tablespoons all-purpose flour
  4 cups stock (or bouillon)
  4 cups water
  2 small carrots, diced
  1 small turnip, diced
  1 stalk celery, diced
  $1/2$ cup barley
  1 cup tomato puree
  2 teaspoons Worcestershire sauce
  1 teaspoon salt
  $1/4$ teaspoon pepper
  $1/8$ teaspoon cayenne pepper
  6 parsley sprigs, chopped
  $1/4$ cup catsup
    juice of $1/4$ lemon

Cut oxtail in small pieces; blanch in water to cover; drain. In same pan with oxtail, place the butter, onion, and garlic; sauté all until browned. Sprinkle with flour and cook again until a good brown color.

Add stock and water; bring to boil; skim. Add carrots, turnip, celery, and barley. Simmer slowly for 2 1/2 hours.

Add tomato puree, Worcestershire, salt, pepper, cayenne pepper, parsley, catsup, and lemon juice. Boil for 10 minutes. Makes 6 servings.

NOTE: Cooks were instructed to "serve in china soup cup underlined with saucer; serve with crackers and butter."

Puget Sound Clam Chowder

> 2 cans (6 1/2 ounces each) minced clams
> 1 1/4-inch cube salt pork, diced
> 1/2 small onion, sliced
> 2 cups potatoes, peeled and
> cut in 3/4-inch cubes
> 1 1/2 teaspoons salt
> 1/8 teaspoon pepper
> 6 tablespoons all-purpose flour
> 1 1/4 cups boiling water
> 2 cups scalded milk
> 3 tablespoons butter
> 4 soda crackers
> cold milk

Drain clams, reserving liquor.

In medium fry pan, fry salt pork; add onion; cook an additional 5 minutes, until onion is tender. Strain off fat. Pour salt pork and onion into stewpot.

In separate pan, parboil potatoes in water to cover for 5 minutes. Drain.

On top of salt pork and onion in stewpot, layer half of the potatoes and half of the salt and pepper; dredge with 2 tablespoons flour. Repeat with the other half of potatoes,

salt, and pepper and 2 tablespoons flour. Add 1 1/4 cups boiling water. Cook slowly for 10 minutes, watching to keep from burning.

Add milk, clams, and 2 tablespoons butter. Cook 3 minutes, stirring occasionally. Soak crackers in just enough milk to moisten. Add crackers to chowder.

Heat reserved clam liquor to boiling. In small pan melt 1 tablespoon butter, then stir in 2 tablespoons flour. Slowly add hot clam liquor.

Add thickened clam liquor to chowder just before serving. Makes 4 servings.

NOTE: Clam liquor is added last because it tends to cause the milk to separate.

Purée of Split Pea Soup

> 1 pound dry split green peas
> water to cover
> 6 cups cold water
> 2 tablespoons butter, or chicken fat
> 1/2 medium onion, sliced
> 1 small carrot, sliced
> 1 small stalk of celery with leaves, chopped
> 1 small clove garlic, finely chopped
> 1/2 small ham hock
> 4 whole cloves
> 1/4 bay leaf
> salt
> pepper

In soup kettle, cover peas with water and let stand overnight. Drain; add 6 cups fresh cold water.

In small frying pan, sauté onion, carrot, celery, and garlic in butter until tender, about 10 minutes.

Continued on p. 124

Add sautéed vegetables, ham hock, cloves, and bay leaf to soup kettle. Season with salt and pepper, to taste. Simmer 1 hour until done, stirring often to prevent scorching. Press through a strainer. Makes 2 quarts.

NOTE: The recipe originally called for using a "China cap," a cone-shaped strainer perhaps so named because it was thought to resemble a hat worn by ancient Chinese scholars.

Bisque of Crab

1/4 pound butter
1 cup minced onions
1/2 cup minced carrots
1/2 cup all-purpose flour
2 cups fish stock (not too strong,
*   made from fish bones and trimmings)*
2 cups milk
2 cans (6 ounces each) crab meat
*   salt*
*   white pepper*
*   cayenne pepper*

Using 3-quart, heavy-bottomed saucepan, melt butter. Add onion and carrots; cook slowly 10 minutes until tender.

Stir in flour; cook 1 minute. Add stock gradually, then add milk; heat to simmering. Stir in crab meat. Season to taste with salt and pepper. Add a little cayenne pepper. Makes 4 servings.

Crab Gumbo Louisiana

2 tablespoons butter
1/2 cup chopped onions
1/4 cup chopped green pepper
4 cups fish broth (made from bones and
*   trimmings of fish)*
1/4 cup long grain rice
1 cup canned tomatoes with juice
1/2 cup okra, drained
1/2 teaspoon Worcestershire sauce
*   salt*
*   pepper*
*   cayenne pepper*
1 can (6 ounces) crab meat

In 3-quart, heavy-bottomed pan, melt butter. Add onions and green pepper; cook 10 minutes until tender.

Add fish broth and rice; boil slowly for 15 minutes.

Add tomatoes, okra, and Worcestershire sauce. Season with salt and pepper to taste; add very little cayenne pepper. Simmer slowly for 1 hour.

Add crab meat; bring to a boil; remove from heat. Serve with crackers and butter. Makes 4 servings.

Bisque of Oysters

1 can (8 ounces) oysters for stew
1 1/2 cups milk
*   bouquet garni consisting of onion, celery, parsley,*
*   thyme, bay leaf, and clove*
1/2 cup cream
2 tablespoons all-purpose flour
*   water or cream*
1/4 teaspoon salt
*   dash of white pepper*
1 tablespoon butter

Drain oysters, reserving 1 cup juice.

In medium saucepan, heat milk; add reserved juice; add bouquet garni. Simmer for 10 minutes.

Remove bouquet garni and strain liquid. Return liquid to cleaned saucepan; add cream; heat.

Mix flour with a little water or cream; simmer soup until consistency of cream. Add oysters and heat 3 to 5 minutes on very low heat. Season with salt and white pepper to taste. Stir in butter. Serve. Makes 4 servings.

Potage Reine Mogador

    6 medium potatoes, chunked
    3 large leeks, sliced
      water
      cream of chicken soup
      salt
      pepper
    1 cup cream
    1 tablespoon butter

In large saucepan, place potatoes and leeks with water to cover. Cook 20 to 30 minutes, until tender. Reserve stock. Pass vegetables through Chinese strainer or food mill.

In large saucepan, pour reserved stock; add water, if necessary, to make 2 quarts. Measure puree of potatoes and leeks and add to stock; add cream of chicken soup in an amount equal to the puree of potatoes and leeks.

Heat. Season with salt and pepper to taste. Just before serving, add cream and butter, holding on heat a few minutes. Makes 3 quarts.

Salads and Salad Dressings

Salmon Salad Delight

    1 can (16 ounces) salmon, drained and flaked
    2 cups chopped celery
    1 cup chopped sweet pickles
    4 hard-cooked eggs, chopped
    1/2 teaspoon salt
    1/2 teaspoon white pepper
    1/8 teaspoon marjoram
      mayonnaise to moisten
      lettuce
      garnish consisting of hard-cooked eggs,
        tomato wedges, lemon wedges, sprigs of parsley,
        mayonnaise, and paprika

In medium bowl, combine the first 7 ingredients. Add just enough mayonnaise to moisten. Chill.

Serve salad in shape of pyramid on lettuce leaf. Garnish each salad with 1/2 of a hard-cooked egg, 1 tomato wedge, 1 lemon wedge, and 1 parsley sprig; place a dash of mayonnaise on top of the pyramid and sprinkle paprika lightly on mayonnaise. As a luncheon salad, makes 4 servings.

Waldorf Salad

For a gourmet delight, use ingredients of the finest quality. The larger Washington Delicious apples are ideal.

> 4 large red apples, cored and diced (do not peel)
> 1/2 cup dark raisins
> 3/4 cup finely chopped crisp celery
> 1/3 cup coarsely chopped walnuts
> 6 tablespoons confectioners' sugar, sifted
> 2/3 to 1 cup mayonnaise (just enough
>   for good consistency)

In medium bowl, place first 4 ingredients. Mix confectioners' sugar with mayonnaise; add to first mixture. Cover and chill for 2 to 3 hours.

Stir well, serve on crisp lettuce leaves. Makes 6 to 8 servings.

Salad Louise

Arrange 4 whole sections of peeled grapefruit on lettuce leaf. Place seedless grapes in center. Cover with spoonful of French Dressing (see below).

French Dressing for Salad Louise

> 1/2 cup orange juice
> 1/2 cup olive oil
> 2 tablespoons honey
> 1 teaspoon salt
> 1/2 teaspoon paprika

Mix well.

Salad Florentine

> 2 cups chopped cabbage
> 3/4 cup diced celery
> 1/4 cup diced cucumber
> 1/4 cup mayonnaise
> 2 hard-boiled eggs, chopped

In medium bowl, combine first 4 ingredients. Mold on lettuce leaf on bread plate. Sprinkle with chopped eggs. Makes 4 servings.

Mixed Cut Green Salad

In salad bowl, combine the following cut vegetables: lettuce, radishes, green onions, celery, cucumber, hearts of artichokes, green pepper. (Use amounts according to personal preference.) Add a few green peas.

Serve with NP French Dressing (see below) on the side.

NP French Dressing

Combine 2 parts vinegar, 1 part olive oil, salt and pepper to taste, and a little garlic. Mix well.

Pearadise Crab Salad

Beautiful! A favorite on the dining cars.

> leaf lettuce
> 3 canned pear halves
> 3 crab legs
> 6 avocado crescents
> 1/2 fresh tomato (peeled)
> salad dressing
> 3 parsley sprigs

On bed of leaf lettuce on luncheon plate, arrange pear halves spokewise. Place crab legs between pear halves. On each side of crab leg, place an avocado crescent.

Make center arrangement of tomato half, cut side down; top with a salad dressing of your choice.

Garnish with parsley sprigs. Makes 1 serving.

Slenderella Salad

lettuce leaves
pear
peach
apple
orange
green seedless grapes, halved
Bing cherries, halved
diced pineapple

Place crisp lettuce leaves on luncheon plate. Slice fresh pear, peach, and apple to match shape of orange sections; alternate in wagon wheel effect on lettuce leaves.

Combine grapes, cherries, and pineapple; place in center of plate. Serve Honey Dressing (see recipe p. 128) on the side.

Fruit Salad Royal

Place 1 slice of pineapple on crisp lettuce leaf on plate. Cut a thick slice of a large orange and place on pineapple. Top with 3 or 4 slices of banana.

Cover salad with dressing made of half whipped cream and half mayonnaise. Sprinkle with minced maraschino cherries and mint leaves (or cherries and nuts). Makes 1 serving.

Diplomat Salad

pineapple
celery
apple
mayonnaise
lettuce
chopped walnuts
maraschino cherries

Cut equal parts of pineapple, celery, and apple in julienne shape. Mix with mayonnaise, just enough to moisten.

Serve on lettuce leaf. Sprinkle with chopped walnuts. Garnish with 1/2 maraschino cherry in center, flat side down.

Bartlett Pear en Surprise

Serve 1/2 pear per salad. Place pear half on lettuce leaf; fill center of pear with cottage cheese.

Cover with dressing made of half whipped cream and half mayonnaise. Place maraschino cherry on top and sprinkle with chopped nuts.

Fruit Cup Honolulu

Use equal parts orange and pineapple. Cut in 1/2-inch cubes. Chill thoroughly.

Serve in cocktail glass. Sprinkle with chopped walnuts.

Russian Dressing

1 cup mayonnaise
1/4 cup chile or cocktail sauce
1 teaspoon chopped pimientos
2 ripe or green olives, chopped
1 teaspoon Worcestershire sauce
olive oil
vinegar
salt
pepper

Place mayonnaise in a medium bowl. Add next 4 ingredients.

Thin to proper consistency with equal parts olive oil and vinegar. Season with a little salt and pepper to taste. Chill. Makes 1 1/3 cups.

NOTE: Tester used 1 teaspoon each of olive oil and vinegar.

Honey Dressing for Fruit

1 1/3 cups mayonnaise
1/2 cup honey
paprika

Stir mayonnaise until smooth. Add honey and mix well. Sprinkle with paprika; stir. Serve with fruit. Makes 1 3/4 cups.

1000 Island Dressing

2 cups mayonnaise
1/8 medium-sized green pepper, chopped
1 tablespoon chopped stuffed olives
1 tablespoon chopped pimientos
1/4 cup pickle relish
1/2 cup chili sauce

In medium bowl, place all ingredients. Blend thoroughly. Chill. Makes 3 cups.

"Our Own" French Dressing

This NP French dressing was bottled and sold to dining car patrons.

2 medium eggs
6 tablespoons sugar
1/4 cup catsup
1 tablespoon dry mustard
2 1/2 tablespoons paprika
4 cups salad oil
2 1/2 tablespoons salt
1 cup tarragon vinegar
1/4 cup lemon juice

In large bowl, whip eggs for several minutes, until well beaten.

In small bowl, mix sugar, catsup, dry mustard, and paprika with a little of the salad oil; add to the eggs slowly, beating well. Add remaining salad oil gradually. Add salt; add vinegar and lemon juice slowly, beating constantly. Makes 1 1/2 quarts.

Parisienne Dressing

Serve on tomatoes.

> 1/2 cup finely diced celery
> 1 tablespoon minced onions
> 1 anchovy, minced
>   a little minced garlic
>   salt
>   pepper
>   chopped parsley
> 1 tablespoon vinegar
> 2 tablespoons vegetable oil

In small bowl, combine first 4 ingredients. Season with salt and pepper to taste; sprinkle with chopped parsley.

Pour vinegar and oil over ingredients in bowl; mix well. Chill dressing 2 hours. Makes 4 servings.

Cottage Cheese Dressing

Whip cottage cheese. Thin with cream to desired consistency. Add a little lemon juice; beat well. Add a few chopped toasted almonds.

Fish and Seafoods

Broiled Salmon St. Germain

A real treat. Serve with Béarnaise Sauce.

Cut salmon into 4-ounce fillets. Season with salt and pepper. Dip in melted butter and roll in fresh bread crumbs; place in baking dish. Bake at 400 degrees until brown and done, about 15 minutes.

Serve on plate and cover with Béarnaise Sauce (see recipe p. 138). Garnish with lemon, parsley, and Parisienne Potatoes (see recipe p. 143).

Baked Haddock Fillets with Puffy Cheese Sauce

> 2 pounds haddock fillets
>   salt
>   pepper

Thaw frozen fillets. Cut into serving-size portions. Salt and pepper to taste. Place fillets in a single layer in a well-greased, 9-by-13-inch baking pan.

Cover fish with Puffy Cheese Sauce (see below). Bake at 350 degrees for 30 minutes, or until fish flakes easily when tested with a fork and the sauce is brown. Serve immediately. Makes 6 servings.

Puffy Cheese Sauce

> 1/4 cup mayonnaise, or salad dressing
> 1 tablespoon chopped sweet pickle or pickle relish
> 1/4 cup grated cheese
> 2 egg yolks, beaten
> 2 egg whites, beaten

In medium bowl, combine mayonnaise, sweet pickle, cheese, and egg yolks. Fold in egg whites.

Gulf Shrimp Creole with Rice

1 cup long grain rice
2 cups water
1 teaspoon salt
1 teaspoon cooking oil
4 tablespoons butter
1 package (6 ounces) frozen cooked shrimp,
  thawed and drained

In 2-quart saucepan, combine rice, water, salt, and cooking oil. Bring to a rolling boil, then lower heat. Cover and simmer for 15 minutes.

In medium saucepan, melt butter. Add shrimp; sauté. Add 3 cups hot Creole Sauce (see recipe p. 140), hold on heat 1 minute.

Place a mound of hot rice in center of plate. Pour shrimp with sauce over and around mound. Makes 4 servings.

Fillet of Pike with Tartar Sauce

Wash 2 pounds pike fillets in cold water; dry. Season with salt and pepper. Dip in flour, then in 1 beaten egg mixed with 2 to 3 tablespoons water, then in flour again. Fry in 1/2 inch fat. Garnish with parsley and quarter of lemon. Serve Tartar Sauce (see below) separately.

Tartar Sauce

Combine chopped dill pickle, capers, minced onion, and chopped parsley, 1/2 cup in all, proportions to taste. Squeeze out surplus juice. Mix with 1 cup mayonnaise. Chill.

Pike Marinade

Place 2 pounds pike fillets in single layer in 9-by-13-inch baking dish. Pour 1/2 cup vegetable oil over fillets. Sprinkle with salt, pepper, and chopped parsley. Place slices of 1 small onion and 1 small lemon on top of fillets. Steep for 2 hours, turning occasionally.

Drain off oil, retaining other marinade ingredients. Add 1 cup fish broth (made from bones and trimmings of fish) and 4 ounces of white wine (or to taste). Sprinkle pieces of butter on top. Bake at 300 degrees for 40 minutes, basting frequently.

Strain gravy, then reduce it. Thicken slightly with a mixture of a little flour and water. Add some essence of anchovy, a few tablespoons of butter, and some capers. Pour over fish.

Fillet of Halibut Mornay

Cut 2 pounds halibut fillets into serving-sized pieces. Place in saucepan with water to cover; season with salt and pepper to taste. Simmer gently until nearly done, about 8 to 10 minutes.

Place fillets in buttered serving dish; cover with Mornay Sauce (see recipe p. 138). Sprinkle with Parmesan cheese and melted butter. Bake in oven until brown.

Serve on dinner plate with Potatoes Duchesse (see recipe p. 142). Garnish with thin slice of lemon and parsley sprig.

Fillet of Halibut Cubaine

Cut 2 pounds halibut fillets into serving-size pieces. Dredge in flour; sauté in butter until done.

Place on dinner plate, cover with Creole Sauce (see recipe p. 140). Serve a mound of boiled rice on the side.

Boiled Halibut with Shrimp Sauce

In large saucepan, cover 2 to 3 pounds halibut steaks with water. Add slice of lemon, salt, pepper, and bouquet garni (made of parsley, bay leaf, thyme, and clove). Simmer gently for 8 to 10 minutes, until done.

Make a rich cream sauce using 4 tablespoons butter, 4 tablespoons flour, 2 cups milk, and 1 egg yolk; add ½ cup chopped, cooked shrimp. Season with cayenne pepper to taste.

Place halibut steaks on dinner plate, pour some shrimp sauce over each. Garnish with chopped white and yolk of hard-boiled egg.

Tomato Stuffed with Crab Meat

4 tomatoes
½ cup canned crab meat, drained
½ cup finely chopped celery
2 tablespoons mayonnaise

Scald tomatoes by pouring boiling water over them. After about 30 seconds dip tomatoes in ice water; peel. Chill thoroughly. Slice off tops of tomatoes; cut out centers.

In small bowl, combine crab meat, celery, and mayonnaise. Fill each tomato with ¼ of the mixture. Serve on lettuce leaf. Makes 4 servings.

Meats

NP Irish Stew

2 pounds boneless shoulder of lamb
1 stalk celery with leaves, diced
1 medium onion, chopped
1 medium potato, sliced in ¼-inch slices
2 cups hot water (3 if needed to cover)
2 ¼ teaspoons salt
¼ teaspoon pepper
dash ground thyme
6 medium whole potatoes
12 small whole onions
2 tablespoons all-purpose flour
2 tablespoons cold water
chopped parsley for garnish

Trim and cube lamb. Place in Dutch oven or heavy 4-quart saucepan. Add celery, chopped onion, sliced potato, hot water, salt, pepper, and thyme. Cover and simmer over low heat for 1 hour.

Place whole potatoes and whole onions atop meat. Cover and cook 40 minutes longer. Remove potatoes and onions; set aside.

Blend flour and cold water; add to cooking liquid; cook until thickened for gravy.

Put meat in center of warm serving platter. Surround with whole potatoes and onions. Garnish potatoes with chopped parsley. Serve remaining gravy separately in gravy boat. Makes 6 servings.

VARIATION: Other vegetables such as carrots, turnips, and peas may be added.

Hawaiian Pot Roast

A very flavorful pot roast. Do not add salt—it is in the soy sauce.

    4 pounds arm or blade cut of beef
    2 tablespoons lard or drippings
    1/4 cup soy sauce
    3/4 cup hot water
    1/4 teaspoon pepper
    1/4 teaspoon ground ginger
    1 medium onion, sliced
    3/4 cup mushroom pieces
    1/2 cup sliced celery
    1 can (8 ounces) pineapple chunks
    2 tablespoons all-purpose flour
    1/4 cup cold water

Brown pot roast in lard or drippings. Pour off fat. Add soy sauce, hot water, pepper, ginger, and onion. Cover tightly and simmer over low heat approximately 2 hours.

Add mushrooms, celery, and pineapple; continue cooking for another 20 minutes. Celery should remain slightly crisp. Remove meat, vegetables, and pineapple; keep warm.

Blend flour and cold water; add to cooking liquid; cook until thickened. Stir vegetables and pineapple into thickened sauce. Serve portion of sauce with sliced beef. Makes 8 servings.

NOTE: If you are not a lover of soy sauce, use less.

Veal Schnitzel

    6 veal cutlets
    paprika
    salt
    pepper
    all-purpose flour
    1 egg, beaten
    fresh bread crumbs
    hot tomato sauce
    6 lemon slices
    6 anchovies
    6 capers

Season cutlets with paprika, salt, and pepper to taste. Roll in flour, dip in beaten egg, then roll in bread crumbs. Fry to a rich brown. Serve with tomato sauce.

Garnish tops by placing 1 slice of lemon on center of each cutlet; top lemon with anchovy rolled with caper inside. Makes 6 servings.

Swiss Steak with Brown Sauce

    2 1/2 pounds beef round steak
    1 teaspoon salt
    1/4 teaspoon pepper
    1/2 cup all-purpose flour
    3 tablespoons bacon fat
    1 large onion, thinly sliced
    2 stalks celery, sliced
    1/2 small green pepper, diced
    1 can (16 ounces) tomatoes
    1 cup beef stock
    flour
    cold water

Sprinkle half of salt, pepper, and flour on one side of round steak. Pound well with meat mallet. Do same to second side. Cut in serving-size pieces.

Brown steaks in bacon fat in medium-hot skillet for 2 to 3 minutes each side. Add onion, celery, and pepper; braise for 15 minutes. Add tomatoes and beef stock. Bake at 300 degrees until done, about 1 hour.

Remove steaks from skillet; set aside and keep warm. Combine a little flour and cold water; add to sauce in skillet; cook until thickened.

To serve, place piece of steak on plate, pour some of thickened brown sauce from skillet over steak. Makes 5 servings.

Roast Beef with Yorkshire Pudding

> *1 beef roast (5 to 6 pounds)*
> *salt*
> *pepper*
> *Yorkshire Pudding (see below)*

Place beef roast in roasting pan; sprinkle with salt and pepper. Roast at 325 degrees until it reaches desired doneness. Spoon off drippings for use in Yorkshire Pudding. Serve slices with Yorkshire Pudding.

Yorkshire Pudding

> *4 eggs*
> *1 cup milk*
> *2 cups all-purpose flour, sifted*
> *1 teaspoon salt*
> *²/₃ cup hot beef drippings (if insufficient beef drippings, add melted butter to make ²/₃ cup), divided*

In medium bowl, combine eggs, milk, flour, salt, and ¹/₃ cup beef drippings. Beat for 2 to 3 minutes, until mixture is smooth.

Pour remaining ¹/₃ cup beef drippings in 8-inch-square baking pan, or divide among 10 heated custard cups, as desired.

Pour pudding mixture in pan or custard cups; bake at 400 degrees until browned, approximately 30 minutes. Makes 10 servings.

New England Boiled Dinner

> *¹/₂ pound salt pork*
> *1 corned beef brisket (3 to 4 pounds)*
> *   water*
> *3 large turnips, quartered*
> *6 large carrots, cut in 2-inch chunks*
> *6 medium potatoes, quartered*
> *1 small head cabbage, quartered*
> *3 large beets, quartered*
> *   chopped parsley for garnish*

Place salt pork in soup kettle and cover with cold water. Bring to a boil several times, changing water each time. After freshening in this manner, drain and add corned beef; cover with fresh cold water. Bring to a boil; skim; reduce to low heat. Simmer until both are tender, 3 to 3 ¹/₂ hours. Remove meats and keep warm.

Add turnips, carrots, potatoes, and cabbage to liquid in soup kettle. Bring to boil, reduce heat, and cook about 30 minutes, until vegetables are tender. Cook beets in separate, medium kettle until tender.

Serve in casserole, arranging with cabbage in center, a slice of corned beef and a slice of salt pork over the cabbage, and one each of the other vegetables around the side. Garnish with a little chopped parsley. Makes 6 servings.

Baked Rabbit Pie

1 large rabbit, cut in pieces
2 cups water
3 tablespoons butter
¼ cup chopped onions
2 parsley sprigs, chopped
½ cup chopped mushrooms
4 tablespoons all-purpose flour
¼ cup white wine
⅛ teaspoon pepper
⅛ teaspoon salt
dash ground nutmeg
1 tablespoon lemon juice
1 pie shell (9-inch), baked
1 pastry cover (7-inch), baked

In large, heavy-bottomed saucepan, place rabbit and water. Bring to a boil, lower heat, and cook for 30 minutes. Drain rabbit, reserving 1 cup broth. Remove rabbit from bones and cut in small pieces.

In same saucepan, melt butter; add cut-up rabbit. Sauté rabbit for 5 minutes. Add onion, parsley, and mushrooms; sauté 5 minutes longer.

Stir in flour. Add wine, 1 cup reserved broth, pepper, salt, and nutmeg. Cook 30 minutes or until rabbit is tender. Stir in lemon juice. Pour into prepared pie shell and top with pastry cover. Makes one 9-inch pie.

VARIATION: Cook small amounts of carrots and potatoes separately; add during the last 5 minutes.

Broiled Ham Steak Florida

Broil ham steak.

Flour and fry pineapple rings in butter; cut in half.

Cook sweet potatoes with skins on, peel, and cut in half; fry in butter.

For each serving, place ham steak on dinner plate; arrange 2 halves of pineapple and 1 half of sweet potato around ham.

Escalloped Potatoes with Ham

Place slices of ham (not too small) in bottom of greased baking dish. Add a layer of thinly sliced potatoes, then one of sliced onions, seasoning each layer with salt and pepper to taste. Repeat potato and onion layers. Then place more slices of ham on top. Barely cover with milk. Bake at 350 degrees until done, about 50 to 60 minutes.

Little Pig Sausages, Pineapple, and Sweet Potatoes

Fry little pig (link) sausages until golden brown.

Lightly flour 2 pineapple rings and fry in butter.

Cook sweet potatoes for 20 minutes or until tender; peel; slice crosswise in ¼-inch slices; brown in butter.

Serve 2 pineapple rings on a plate; top each with a slice of sweet potato; top each sweet potato with 2 little pig sausages. Garnish with parsley.

Salisbury Steak

Season ground beef with salt and pepper; add a little chopped onion. Mix in about 2 tablespoons cream to each ¾ pound of meat. Mold into oval steaks.

Roll in fresh bread crumbs; dip in oil. Broil until done to your choice. Garnish with Banana Scallops (see recipe p. 155), slice of lemon, and parsley sprigs.

Native Buffalo Steak

Rub a little lemon juice on both sides of a buffalo steak. Season to taste with salt, pepper, and paprika. Cook steak quickly on both sides in hot pan with butter.

Garnish with slice of fried tomato, ¹/₂ slice fried eggplant, 2 fresh mushroom caps, and ¹/₂ slice bacon.

NOTE: Even if you prefer rare beef, you may want to cook this longer.

Poultry and Stuffings

Chicken and Vegetable Stew

    1 fricassée chicken (4 to 5 pounds)
    3 tablespoons shortening
    2 cups hot water
    1 tablespoon salt
    ³/₄ teaspoon pepper
    12 small white onions
    1 cup fresh carrots, sliced
    1 cup fresh peas, lima beans, or snap beans
    1 cup diced potatoes
    ¹/₃ cup all-purpose flour
    ¹/₂ cup cold water
       few drops Kitchen Bouquet (optional)

Cut chicken in serving-sized pieces; brown on all sides in hot shortening.

Place in Dutch oven or saucepan with hot water, salt, and pepper. Cover and cook 1 hour, or until chicken is tender; add vegetables about 30 minutes before cooking time is up.

Combine flour with cold water; stir into stew. Cook until medium thick. If desired, add a few drops of Kitchen Bouquet to give the sauce a rich, brown color. Makes 6 servings.

Chicken Pot Pie Parisienne

    1 frying chicken (2 ¹/₂ pounds)
    1 ¹/₂ teaspoons salt
    ¹/₄ teaspoon pepper
    1 small onion, diced
    1 stalk celery, diced
    2 cups water
    2 carrots, Parisienne cut
    2 medium potatoes, Parisienne cut
    ¹/₄ cup button mushrooms
    ¹/₄ cup peas
    3 tablespoons all-purpose flour
    ³/₄ cup half-and-half

Place chicken, salt, pepper, onion, and celery in large kettle with water. Bring to a boil; reduce heat and simmer, covered, for 35 minutes. Reserve liquid and cool chicken.

Remove and discard skin and bones; cut chicken in 1-inch pieces.

Using reserved liquid, cook remaining vegetables about 10 minutes, until almost tender. Remove vegetables from liquid.

To make gravy, blend flour and half-and-half; add to cooking liquid. Gravy should have consistency of cream.

Place equal parts of light and dark meat in 4 individual casseroles; add vegetables to each; pour the rich gravy over

Continued on p.136

all. Cover with biscuit or pastry top. Cut steam vents in top and bake at 350 degrees for 1 hour. Makes 4 individual chicken pot pies.

NOTE: You may wish to top with puff paste, which was used in a 1948 NP recipe.

Fried Spring Chicken, Southern Style

1 broiler chicken (2 pounds)
salt
pepper
all-purpose flour
2 tablespoons oil
parsley sprigs for garnish

Cut chicken in quarters. Season with salt and pepper to taste; roll in flour. In large fry pan, fry chicken uncovered to deep golden brown on both sides. Finish cooking in covered pan on stove or in 350-degree oven; total cooking time should be about 1 hour.

Make cream gravy from pan drippings, adding flour for thickening, milk, and salt and pepper to taste. To serve, place 2 quarters of chicken on toast; pour cream gravy over chicken; garnish with parsley. Makes 2 servings.

Whole Squab Chicken, Parisienne

Wash Rock Cornish game hens, 1 to 1 ½ pounds each; dry. Stuff with stuffing of your choice (see recipes). Place in open roasting pan and roast for 30 minutes at 425 degrees. Pour a ladle of consommé over the hens; cover; reduce heat to 350 degrees and roast 45 minutes longer, until done but not dry.

Place each hen in a separate casserole. Make gravy by adding a little stock to drippings; thicken with all-purpose flour and pour around each hen. Add cooked vegetables to each: 3 balls of potatoes and 3 balls of carrots cut with Parisienne cutter (or melon scoop), 3 button mushrooms, and a teaspoon of peas. Serve 1 game hen per person.

Roast Young Turkey

Remove all pin feathers from turkey, clean thoroughly, and stuff with Chestnut Stuffing (see recipe p. 137). Tie the legs; place turkey in roaster with some chopped onions and carrots and a bay leaf. Brush with melted butter.

Brown well, continuing to baste until done. Remove turkey from pan. Remove bay leaf and surplus fat from drippings in pan. Make gravy by adding a little stock to drippings; thicken with all-purpose flour. Season with salt and pepper to taste.

Roast Young Duckling

Rinse duckling inside and out with cold water; dry thoroughly. Sprinkle cavity with salt and pepper to taste. Fill with Peanut Stuffing (see recipe p. 137).

Place duck, breast side up, on rack in shallow pan. Roast in 400-degree oven until done. If duck is larger than 3 pounds, reduce temperature to 325 degrees after 1 hour.

Pour off excess fat and make gravy, if desired, by adding a little stock to drippings; thicken with all-purpose flour. Serve ½ duck per person.

Peanut Stuffing

> 4 cups dry bread crumbs
> 1 onion, minced
> 2 teaspoons salt (1 teaspoon if using salted peanuts)
> 1/2 teaspoon paprika
>   dash of cayenne pepper
> 3/4 cup beef drippings or melted butter
> 2 cups blanched peanuts, chopped
> 1 cup milk
> 1 cup cream

In medium bowl, combine bread crumbs with onion, salt, paprika, and cayenne pepper. Add beef drippings or melted butter; stir in peanuts. Add milk and cream. If stuffing is too dry, add a little more milk. Stuffs 4 ducks.

NOTE: You may wish to use fewer peanuts.

Chestnut Stuffing

> 1 cube (3/4-inch) salt pork, finely diced
> 1 1/2 cups chopped onions
> 3/4 cup chopped celery
> 2 chicken livers, finely diced
> 1 parsley sprig, chopped
> 2 1/2 teaspoons salt
> 1/2 teaspoon pepper
> 1 small clove garlic, minced
> 1/16 teaspoon ground thyme
> 12 cups fresh crumbed bread
> 1 can (8 ounces) water chestnuts

In medium fry pan, place diced salt pork, onions, and celery. Simmer 5 minutes. Add diced chicken livers, parsley, salt, pepper, garlic, and thyme; simmer until done.

In large bowl, place bread crumbs. Add ingredients from fry pan; stir well. Add water chestnuts. Stuffs 16-pound turkey.

Celery and Walnut Stuffing

> 1 cup butter
> 1 cup chopped onions
> 1 cup chopped parsley
> 2 cups chopped celery
> 12 cups day-old bread cubes
> 1 tablespoon salt
> 1/2 teaspoon pepper
> 3 eggs, slightly beaten
> 1/2 cup cool water
> 1 cup chopped walnuts

In medium fry pan, simmer butter, onions, parsley, and celery for 5 minutes.

In large mixing bowl, place bread cubes; add salt and pepper. Add simmered vegetables and mix well.

Stir water into beaten eggs; add to bread cubes. Add walnuts; toss until well mixed. Stuffs 16-pound turkey.

Thyme Stuffing

Dice some onion fine; sauté in butter until done, but do not brown. Add onion to desired amount of freshly mashed potatoes.

Season with small amounts of ground thyme and ground nutmeg, chopped parsley, and white pepper and salt to taste. Whip potatoes.

Place potatoes in baking pan; sprinkle with melted butter. Brown in oven.

Continued on p. 138

Serve with duck: place a serving of thyme dressing on dinner plate; arrange carved duck on top. Pour a spoonful of duck gravy over all. Garnish with parsley.

Sage Stuffing

  2 medium onions, chopped
  1/4 cup minced bacon
  1/2 cup meat fat (see Note)
  1/4 cup butter
  12 cups dry bread crumbs
  1 1/2 teaspoons rubbed sage
  1/8 teaspoon ground nutmeg
  1/4 teaspoon pepper
  1 teaspoon salt
  3/4 cup cream

Sauté onions and minced bacon in meat fat and butter. In large bowl, place bread crumbs; stir in spices. Pour sautéed onions and bacon over bread crumbs; mix well. Add cream. Use no other liquid. Stuffs 16-pound turkey.

NOTE: "Meat fat" was probably whatever the cook had available at the time—for example, leaf lard or rendered suet.

Sauces

Béarnaise Sauce

  1 clove garlic, minced
  1/2 large onion, finely chopped
  1/2 cup vinegar
    juice of 1/2 lemon
  2 cups milk
  1/2 cup all-purpose flour
  6 tablespoons butter
  4 egg yolks, beaten
    chopped parsley
    ground cayenne pepper

In medium saucepan, combine garlic, onion, vinegar, and lemon juice; simmer until liquid is reduced to half.

In separate medium saucepan, melt butter and stir in flour; add milk all at once; cook until thick. Add egg yolks. Do not boil.

Add sauce to pan with onions. Stir over very low heat for a few minutes. Strain; season with chopped parsley and cayenne pepper, to taste. Sauce should be the consistency of mayonnaise. Makes 3 cups.

Mornay Sauce

  2 cups cream
  2 egg yolks
  1 tablespoon grated cheese
    salt
    cayenne pepper

In small saucepan, heat cream.

In small bowl, beat egg yolks. Beat a little cream into them, then add this mixture to the pan of hot cream. Add grated cheese; stir until cheese melts. Season to taste with salt and cayenne pepper. Makes 2 ¼ cups.

Bordelaise Sauce

> 4 tablespoons butter, divided
> 2 tablespoons all-purpose flour
> 2 cups beef stock (or rich bouillon)
>   dash of pepper
> 2 tablespoons minced shallots
> ½ cup minced mushrooms

In medium, heavy-bottomed saucepan, melt 2 tablespoons butter; add flour. Stir and cook until flour turns a light brown color. Add beef stock; cook 3 to 5 minutes. Simmer an additional 30 minutes, stirring occasionally. Strain.

In small fry pan, melt remaining 2 tablespoons of butter. Add shallots and mushrooms; sauté 5 minutes. Add to strained brown sauce; simmer 10 minutes. Makes 1 ¼ cups.

Horseradish Sauce

> 3 tablespoons butter
> 3 tablespoons all-purpose flour
> 2 cups hot strained beef broth
> ¼ cup cream
> ¼ cup grated horseradish
>   salt
>   pepper
> 2 teaspoons lemon juice

In 1-quart, heavy-bottomed saucepan, melt butter. Stir in flour; cook over medium heat until mixture is medium brown, stirring constantly.

Gradually stir in hot beef broth; add cream. Simmer a few minutes, until mixture thickens. Season with salt and pepper, to taste. Add lemon juice. Add horseradish (if using bottled horseradish, first drain off all the vinegar) and stir well. Makes 2 ½ cups.

Barbecue Sauce for Spareribs

> 4 tablespoons butter (or meat drippings)
> ½ cup chopped onions
> 6 tablespoons all-purpose flour
> 3 cups hot water
> 2 tablespoons beef bouillon
> 2 tablespoons Worcestershire sauce
> ⅓ cup cider vinegar
> 1 cup tomato catsup
> 2 tablespoons prepared mustard

In 3-quart, heavy-bottomed saucepan, melt butter. Add onions and cook, covered, until onions are tender.

Add flour and stir until golden brown. Add water; heat to boiling and stir in bouillon. Then add remaining ingredients. Bring to boil, reduce heat, cover, and simmer for 15 minutes. Makes 1 quart.

Creole Sauce

    3 tablespoons butter
    1 small clove garlic
    ⅛ teaspoon salt
    1 small onion, finely sliced
    1 small green pepper, finely sliced
    1 can (3 ounces) sliced mushrooms
    2 ounces chopped pimientos
    1 can (16 ounces) tomatoes
    ⅛ teaspoon pepper

    In 3-quart saucepan, melt butter. Chop garlic fine with salt. Add to butter; sauté. Add onion and green pepper and simmer until tender (about 5 minutes). Add remaining ingredients. Cook slowly for 1 hour, stirring occasionally. Makes 3 cups.

Spanish Sauce

    Piquant sauce. Serve over meat loaf or breaded pork cutlet.

    ½ cup butter or other fat
    ⅓ cup lean ham, minced
    ⅓ cup chopped onions
    ⅓ cup chopped celery
    ⅓ cup chopped raw carrots
    ⅓ cup chopped green pepper
    2 tablespoons chopped chili pepper
    1 small clove garlic, mashed
    1 cup all-purpose flour
  1 ½ quarts brown meat stock (canned, or bouillon)
    1 20-ounce can tomatoes, strained
  12 fresh parsley sprigs
    2 large bay leaves
    4 whole cloves
    1 teaspoon salt
    ¼ teaspoon pepper
    1 teaspoon paprika

    In 3-quart saucepan with thick bottom, fry ham and vegetables in butter until well browned. Blend in flour; brown thoroughly, stirring constantly. Heat stock very hot and combine with strained tomato pulp; add gradually to the browned ham and vegetable mixture, stirring constantly.

    Tie parsley with bay leaves and add with remaining seasonings.

    Allow to simmer gently for at least 30 minutes, stirring occasionally. The longer the sauce simmers the better, as the sauce will mellow and ripen. Remove parsley and bay leaves; strain sauce through fine sieve. Makes 2 quarts.

Cocktail Sauce

1 1/3 cups tomato catsup
1 tablespoon horseradish
1 small green pepper, finely diced
2 teaspoons Worcestershire sauce
2 drops Tabasco sauce
1 teaspoon salt

In medium bowl, combine all ingredients. Makes 1 1/2 cups.

Baked Ham Special Sauce

Until now, our family has enjoyed a plain raisin sauce with ham. After trying this Special Sauce, we agreed it is a real treat.

2 cups orange juice
1/2 cup granulated sugar
1/2 cup white raisins
2 ounces maraschino cherries, quartered
1/2 cup orange marmalade
juice of 1/2 fresh lemon
grated rind of 1 fresh orange
2 tablespoons cornstarch dissolved in 1 tablespoon water

Place the first 7 ingredients in medium saucepan. Bring to a boil over medium heat, stirring occasionally. Remove from heat; stir in dissolved cornstarch.

When ready to serve, reheat in double boiler. If too thick, thin with a little juice from pineapple or maraschino cherries. Makes 3 cups.

Potatoes

NP Great Big Baked Potato

The Northern Pacific used only the U.S. No. 1, Netted Gem Baker variety, grown in Washington (and later in Montana). Beginning in 1909, the NP sent its buyers into the potato harvest fields every October where they spent more than a month selecting the "Big Fellows." A potato had to meet rigid requirements before it could become an NP Great Big Baked Potato. Sorted, graded, and shipped with utmost care, the potatoes were stored so as to be kept in perfect condition.

After washing potatoes, pierce both ends and place in 350-degree oven. Bake 2 hours in fall and winter, 1 1/2 hours in spring and summer. Turn potatoes several times. If potatoes have been stored long, place pan of water in oven to compensate for moisture loss.

Upon removing from oven, gently roll to loosen the meaty part from the skin. Cut from end to end, spread partly open, and serve with large pat of butter placed in center.

Potatoes Ritz

Mealy and delicious—out of the ordinary.

Peel and dice raw potatoes into 1/2-inch cubes. Soak in ice water and thoroughly wash to remove all free starch. Boil in salted water for 10 minutes. Drain.

Sauté potatoes in butter until done and browned. Salt and pepper to taste. When done, potatoes should be brown on all sides and in separate pieces.

German Fried Potatoes

Different from regular French fried potatoes—and delicious. This method affords the use of leftover boiled potatoes.

Boil peeled potatoes; cool. Cut in large pieces, French fried style. Fry in hot, deep fat. Drain well.

Potatoes Rissolé

Peel 8 small new potatoes and trim to olive shape, about 2 inches long and 1 inch in diameter. Boil gently until done, about 10 minutes. Drain well. Using medium skillet, brown in 1 tablespoon butter. Makes 4 servings.

Potatoes Hollandaise

Peel small potatoes and trim to olive shape, about 2 inches long and 1 inch in diameter. Place in salted cold water to cover. Slowly bring to boil and simmer until done (slow cooking prevents breakage). Drain well.

Place in serving dish; pour melted butter over potatoes; sprinkle with chopped parsley.

Potatoes Château

Peel 12 small potatoes and trim to olive shape, about 2 inches long and 1 inch in diameter. Cut in half lengthwise; trim sharp edges a little. Blanch in salted water; drain.

Sauté in butter until golden brown. Season with salt and pepper; serve in vegetable dish. Makes 6 servings.

Potatoes Duchesse

Peel 8 medium potatoes and boil until done. Drain well and allow moisture to evaporate until quite dry. Mash fine to remove all lumps. Mix well with unbeaten yolks of 3 eggs, 4 tablespoons butter, and enough cream to moisten. Season with 1 teaspoon salt; add pepper and ground nutmeg to taste.

Turn onto floured board and shape into cylinders about 3 inches long and 1 inch in diameter. Flatten both ends and mark with a cross, using small knife. Place on baking sheet. Brush with 1 beaten egg white, thinned with 1 tablespoon cream; sprinkle with paprika. Bake at 400 degrees until brown. Garnish with parsley. Makes 8 servings.

Potatoes Persillade

Peel 8 new potatoes and trim to olive shape, about 2 inches long and 1 inch in diameter. Place in cold salted water and bring to a boil, then simmer about 10 minutes. Remove from heat and drain.

In clean pan, place vegetable steamer and add fresh cold water as needed. Place potatoes on steamer, cover pan, and steam 15 minutes, or until potatoes are done. Place in serving dish; garnish with chopped parsley; serve with drawn butter. Makes 4 servings.

Potatoes Bouillon

Peel 8 medium potatoes and cut into even quarters. Cover with cold water and set aside.

Slice 4 strips bacon in one-inch pieces. Place in saucepan; add 1 small onion and 1 stalk of celery cut into fine Julienne strips; sauté in 2 tablespoons butter. When onion is tender add 3 cups beef bouillon (or beef stock) and a little chopped parsley. Adjust seasoning with salt and freshly ground pepper.

Add drained potato quarters to saucepan; cook gently to avoid breakage for 20 minutes, or until done. Serve in vegetable dish with a little of the broth. Makes 8 servings.

Potatoes Brabant

Peel 8 medium potatoes and boil until almost done. Drain well and cool. Dice into ½-inch cubes.

In large frying pan, sauté 2 tablespoons minced onion and 2 tablespoons chopped fresh parsley in 2 tablespoons butter. Add diced potatoes and sauté until golden brown. Makes 8 servings.

Potatoes O'Brien

Pare and boil 6 medium potatoes until just done (a bit of firmness is better). Drain well; dice potatoes. Set aside.

In large skillet, sauté ½ cup diced green pepper and ½ cup chopped mild onions in 2 tablespoons butter. Add potatoes and cook until browned. Add ⅔ cup of cooked chopped pimientos. Season to taste with salt and pepper. Mix well, but avoid mushing as much as possible. Makes 6 servings.

Parisienne Potatoes

Cut desired amount of potatoes with Parisienne cutter (a round vegetable scooping spoon—the same tool used to cut melon balls). Place in cold water; bring to boil. Remove from heat and drain.

Place 2 tablespoons of butter in medium, iron fry pan; put in hot oven to melt butter. Add potatoes to pan, stirring to coat with butter; season with salt and paprika to taste. Bake at 400 degrees about 15 minutes, until brown.

Vegetables

Cauliflower Drawn Butter

1 medium-sized head of cauliflower
¼ cup milk
¾ cup water
¼ teaspoon salt

Separate cauliflower into flowerets and place in saucepan with other ingredients.

Place crust of bread on top to absorb smell of cauliflower. Bring to boil; reduce heat and simmer for approximately 8 minutes, until fork tender. Drain well. Serve with drawn butter. Makes 6 servings.

Cauliflower Polonaise

1 freshly boiled head of cauliflower
1 hard-cooked egg, chopped
salt
pepper
chopped parsley
2 tablespoons butter
½ cup fresh bread crumbs

Boil cauliflower according to directions for Cauliflower Drawn Butter (see above recipe). After draining well, divide into 6 serving dishes. Sprinkle each with ⅙ of the chopped egg, salt and pepper to taste, and some parsley.

Melt butter in heavy-bottomed frying pan; add bread crumbs and stir until brown. Sprinkle spoonful of buttered crumbs over the cauliflower. Makes 6 servings.

Herb Buttered Beets

A recipe for tarragon lovers.

2 cups whole baby beets
1 tablespoon butter
1 teaspoon parsley flakes
1 teaspoon finely chopped onion
¼ teaspoon ground thyme
¼ teaspoon dried tarragon, crushed

Heat beets quickly in pan with a little water.

In separate, small saucepan melt butter. Add parsley, onion, thyme, and tarragon; mix well.

Drain beets; pour herb butter over them, mixing lightly. Serve warm.

Cucumber Salad

Slice cucumbers about an hour before you plan to serve them.

Place sliced cucumbers in jar with salt, ice, and water. Drain and serve on lettuce leaf with "Our Own" French Dressing (see recipe p. 128).

Corn O'Brien

2 tablespoons butter
½ cup minced green pepper
2 cups whole kernel corn, drained
½ cup minced pimientos
salt
pepper

In medium, heavy-bottomed saucepan, melt butter. Add green pepper; sauté 5 minutes.

Add corn and pimientos. Cover; simmer 5 minutes, stirring occasionally. Season with salt and pepper to taste. Makes 4 servings.

Artichoke Hearts

1 can (14 ounces) artichoke hearts
1 finely chopped parsley sprig
3 tablespoons butter

Steam artichoke hearts until hot, about 5 minutes. Place in serving bowl; sprinkle with chopped parsley. Melt butter and pour over the "chokes." Makes 4 servings.

Sliced Tomato, Parisienne

Scald the desired number of tomatoes by pouring boiling water over them. After about 30 seconds dip them in ice water; peel. Chill thoroughly.

Cut in thick slices. Place 1 or 2 slices on a lettuce leaf. On top of tomato, spread a tablespoon of Parisienne Dressing (see recipe p. 129).

Hot Cabbage Slaw

Serve with smoked shoulder or loin of pork.

4 cups finely shredded cabbage
½ cup water
salt
pepper
1 tablespoon vinegar
1 tablespoon butter

In 3-quart, heavy-bottomed saucepan, cook cabbage in water for 15 minutes or until nearly done.

Add salt and pepper to taste; add vinegar; stir. Simmer another 5 minutes, until done. Add butter, stir until melted. Makes 4 servings.

Apples and Sweet Potatoes with Maple Syrup

2 pounds sweet potatoes
1 1/2 pounds baking apples
2 tablespoons butter
3/4 cup maple syrup or maple-flavored syrup
1/16 teaspoon salt

Wash sweet potatoes and cook in a covered saucepan 20 to 30 minutes until tender. Drain; cool slightly; peel. Cut crosswise into slices 1/4-inch thick.

Peel, quarter, and core apples. Slice 1/8 inch thick.

Place half of sweet potatoes in a 2-quart casserole. Top with half the apples, half the butter, and half the syrup mixed with salt. Repeat, using remaining ingredients.

Cover; bake at 350 degrees for 30 minutes. Remove cover and bake 20 minutes. Makes 6 to 8 servings.

Breads

Toast Bread

Texture and flavor perfect for toast. Slice thick for toast or French Toast, thin for toasted sandwiches.

2 packages active dry yeast
3 tablespoons sugar
3/4 cup warm water
1 1/2 cups warm milk
1 tablespoon salt
1 tablespoon dry malt
2 tablespoons shortening
5 to 5 1/2 cups all-purpose flour

In large bowl, combine yeast with sugar and warm water; let stand for 8 to 10 minutes.

Add milk, salt, dry malt, and shortening. With mixer at low speed, mix until blended. Add 3 cups of flour and beat thoroughly. Using a wooden spoon, gradually stir in enough of remaining flour to make a moderately stiff dough.

On floured surface, knead dough until smooth and elastic. Place in greased bowl, turning to grease top. Cover and let rise until doubled, about 40 minutes.

Punch down dough, divide in half; let rest 10 minutes. Form loaves and place in 2 greased 8-by-4-inch pans. Let rise again until doubled, about 35 minutes. Bake at 375 degrees for 40 minutes. Makes 2 loaves.

Whole Wheat Bread

A dense, slightly sweet whole grain bread; very good toasted.

> *3 packages active dry yeast*
> *1 cup warm water*
> *1 cup warm milk*
> *¼ cup honey*
> *½ cup Roman Meal cereal*
> *1 tablespoon salt*
> *3 tablespoons shortening*
> *2 cups whole wheat flour*
> *2 ½ to 3 cups all-purpose flour*

In large bowl, combine yeast with water and milk; let stand 10 minutes.

Add honey, cereal, salt, shortening, and whole wheat flour; mix thoroughly. Stir in flour gradually to form a medium stiff dough.

On floured surface, knead dough until smooth and elastic. Place in greased bowl, turning to grease top. Cover and let rise until doubled, about 45 minutes.

Punch down dough, divide in half; let rest 10 minutes. Form loaves and place in 2 greased 8 ½-by-4 ½-inch pans. Let rise again until doubled, about 40 minutes. Bake at 375 degrees for 30 minutes. Makes 2 loaves.

Raisin Bread

> *2 packages active dry yeast*
> *½ cup warm water*
> *½ cup warm milk*
> *1 egg*
> *2 tablespoons sugar*
> *2 tablespoons shortening*
> *1 ½ teaspoons salt*
> *3 ¼ cups all-purpose flour*
> *½ cup raisins, plumped*

In large bowl, combine yeast with water and milk; let stand 10 minutes.

Add egg, sugar, shortening, salt, and 2 cups flour; beat well. Stir in enough of remaining flour to make a medium stiff dough, then add raisins.

On floured surface, knead dough until smooth and elastic. Place in greased bowl, turning to grease top. Cover and let rise until doubled, about 45 minutes to 1 hour.

Punch down dough, divide in half; let rest 10 minutes. Form loaves, place in 2 greased 8-by-4-inch pans. Let rise again until doubled, about 45 minutes. Bake at 375 degrees for 30 minutes. Makes 2 small loaves.

Rye Bread

> *4 packages active dry yeast*
> *2 cups warm water*
> *4 teaspoons shortening*
> *1 ½ teaspoons salt*
> *1 tablespoon dry malt*
> *½ teaspoon rye flavor*
> *1 ½ teaspoons caramel color*
> *3 tablespoons caraway seed*
> *1 ¾ cups rye flour*
> *3 ½ to 4 cups all-purpose flour*

In large bowl, combine yeast with water; let stand 8 to 10 minutes.

Add rest of ingredients except all-purpose flour, beating well. Add 2 cups all-purpose flour, mixing thoroughly. Gradually stir in enough of remaining flour to make a medium stiff dough.

On floured surface, knead dough until smooth and elastic. Place in greased bowl, turning to grease top. Cover and let rise until doubled, about 45 minutes.

Punch down dough, divide in half; let rest 10 minutes. Form loaves and place in 2 greased 8-by-4-inch pans. Let rise again until doubled, about 45 minutes. Bake at 375 degrees for approximately 30 minutes. Makes 2 loaves.

Dinner Rolls

Dough for these rolls can be refrigerated for up to 72 hours. The pans of uncooked rolls can be removed from the refrigerator as needed, allowed to rise until doubled, and baked as usual.

> 2 packages active dry yeast
> $5/8$ cup warm water
> $5/8$ cup warm milk
> $2/3$ cup sugar
> $1/3$ cup shortening
> 1 tablespoon salt
> 1 egg
> $4\,3/4$ to $5\,1/4$ cups all-purpose flour

In large bowl, combine yeast with water and milk; let stand for 10 minutes.

Add sugar, shortening, salt, egg, and 2 cups of flour; beat thoroughly. Using a wooden spoon, gradually stir in enough of remaining flour to make a moderately stiff dough.

On floured surface, knead dough until smooth and elastic. Place in greased bowl, turning to grease top. Cover and let rise until doubled, about $1\,1/2$ to 2 hours.

Punch down dough. Shape dough into $1\,3/4$-inch balls. Place rolls with sides nearly touching in a greased 9-by-13-inch baking pan. Let rise again until doubled, about 1 hour. Bake at 375 degrees for 18 to 20 minutes. Makes $2\,1/2$ dozen rolls.

Dumplings

> 1 egg
> 1 tablespoon butter, melted
> $1/4$ teaspoon salt
> 1 cup milk
> 2 cups all-purpose flour
> 1 tablespoon baking powder

Whip egg, butter, and salt. Add milk, flour, and baking powder. Mix quickly and do not handle any more than necessary.

Roll out on floured board to $1/2$-inch thickness. Cut with 2-inch biscuit cutter.

Lay dumplings atop stew of your choice as it bubbles. Cover; let stew return to boiling. Reduce heat; simmer until done, about 12 to 15 minutes. Remove with slotted spoon. Makes 10 dumplings.

Banana Nut Bread

¹/₃ cup shortening
²/₃ cup sugar
2 eggs
1 ³/₄ cups sifted all-purpose flour
¹/₂ teaspoon salt
2 ³/₄ teaspoons baking powder
1 cup mashed ripe bananas
¹/₂ cup chopped English walnuts

Cream together shortening and sugar. Add eggs and beat well.

Sift together flour, salt, and baking powder. Add to creamed mixture alternately with mashed bananas, blending well after each addition. Stir in walnuts.

Pour into a well-greased 9-by-5-inch loaf pan. Bake at 350 degrees about 50 minutes. Remove from pan; cool completely on rack. Wrap and store overnight for full flavor. Makes 1 loaf.

Fruit Cakes

NP Dark Fruit Cake

Passengers could order whole fruit cakes, famous across the country, from the dining car steward. In 1949 the NP sold 4,004 3-pound cakes and 637 5-pound cakes, for a total of more than 7 ¹/₂ tons.

2 pounds seedless raisins
2 pounds currants
1 pound mixed glazed fruits, sliced
1 pound glazed whole cherries
1 pound candied pineapple, diced
2 ¹/₄ cups granulated sugar
2 cups butter
¹/₂ teaspoon salt
1 teaspoon ground cinnamon
1 teaspoon ground mace
1 teaspoon ground nutmeg
1 teaspoon ground cardamom
12 eggs
1 tablespoon lemon extract
1 tablespoon vanilla extract
1 tablespoon sherry or port wine
5 cups all-purpose flour
1 cup walnuts, halves or pieces
1 cup pecan halves
1 cup whole almonds, blanched

Mix raisins, currants, mixed fruits, cherries, and pineapple the day before cooking and keep in a cool place to blend flavors.

Grease four 9 ¹/₂-by-5 ¹/₄-inch bread pans; line bottoms and sides with strips of heavy brown paper, grease paper.

Lightly cream sugar, butter, and salt. Add spices. Slowly stir in eggs gradually to blend; add extracts and wine. Then add flour, mixing lightly. Add fruits and nuts; combine well.

Pour into prepared pans, filling them ³/₄ full. Bake at 300 degrees approximately 1 hour and 45 minutes. Cool thoroughly; remove from pans. Makes about 10 pounds.

NOTE: Since oven temperatures vary, watch closely—do not overbake.

NP Light Fruit Cake

Although not as well known as the NP Dark Fruit Cake, the light one was preferred by many.

    1 pound glazed pineapple, diced
    1 pound glazed green cherries
    1 pound glazed red cherries
    2 pounds white seedless raisins
    2 pounds mixed glazed fruits, sliced
 2 ³/₄ cups granulated sugar
 1 ¹/₄ cups shortening
    1 cup butter
    1 teaspoon salt
    5 cups all-purpose flour, divided
12 eggs
    1 tablespoon vanilla extract
    1 tablespoon lemon extract
    1 teaspoon ground mace
    1 cup pecan halves
    1 cup walnuts, halves or pieces
    1 cup almonds, blanched

    Mix pineapple, cherries, raisins, and mixed fruits the day before cooking and keep in a cool place to blend flavors.

    Grease four 9 ¹/₂-by-5 ¹/₄-inch bread pans; line bottoms and sides with strips of heavy brown paper, grease paper.

    In rotary mixer, lightly cream sugar, shortening, butter, salt, and 2 ¹/₂ cups flour. Stir in eggs gradually, blending for about 10 minutes. Add extracts, mace, and remaining flour, mixing lightly about 2 minutes. Add fruits and nuts; combine well.

    Pour into prepared pans, filling pans ³/₄ full. Bake at 300 degrees about 1 hour and 45 minutes. Cool thoroughly; remove from pans. Makes 4 loaves or approximately 10 pounds.

    NOTE: Since oven temperatures vary, watch closely—do not overbake.

Pies

Pineapple Cream Pie

    1 can (20 ounces) crushed pineapple with juice
³/₄ cup warm water
    1 cup sugar
    1 tablespoon butter
¹/₂ small lemon (juice and grated rind)
    4 tablespoons cornstarch dissolved in
        3 tablespoons cold water
    2 tablespoons cold water
    2 eggs, separated
    1 pie shell (10-inch), baked
    1 cup whipping cream
    3 teaspoons sugar
    1 teaspoon vanilla

    In 3-quart, heavy-bottomed saucepan, combine pineapple and juice, ³/₄ cup warm water, sugar, butter, and lemon juice and rind. Bring to a boil over medium-high heat, stirring occasionally.

    When mixture starts to boil, thicken with dissolved cornstarch. Lower heat, cook a few minutes until clear, stirring constantly.

Continued on p. 150

Beat egg yolks with 2 tablespoons cold water. Remove hot mixture from stove and stir egg yolks into it, stirring fast and well. Return to stove and stir while holding on low heat for 2 minutes—do not boil. Cool slightly.

In small mixing bowl, beat egg whites to a stiff froth. Fold into cooked mixture.

Pour filling into cooled pie shell. Cool completely.

In medium bowl, beat whipping cream until soft peaks form; add sugar and vanilla; continue beating until stiff peaks form.

Just before serving, cover pie with whipped cream.

Lemon Chiffon Pie

Many of you will remember the Northern Pacific individual pies with meringue piled high—higher than you had seen anywhere before or since.

> 2 cups warm water
> 1 1/4 cups sugar
>   pinch of salt
> 7 tablespoons lemon juice (or juice of 2 large lemons)
>   grated rind of 1 1/2 lemons
> 6 tablespoons cornstarch dissolved in 1/2 cup cold water
> 3 egg yolks, slightly beaten
> 1 tablespoon butter
> 5 egg whites (at room temperature)
> 1/4 teaspoon salt
> 1/4 teaspoon cream of tartar
> 10 tablespoons sugar
> 1 pie shell (10-inch), baked

Place warm water, sugar, salt, and lemon juice and rind in heavy 2-quart saucepan; bring to a boil.

Add dissolved cornstarch to egg yolks. When first mixture comes to a boil, remove from heat and add egg yolk mixture all at once, stirring vigorously. Return to heat and cook until thickened (it will thicken more as it cools), stirring constantly. Remove from heat and stir in butter.

Prepare meringue by placing egg whites, salt, and cream of tartar in bowl. Beat at high speed until frothy. Quickly add sugar, 1 tablespoon at a time. Continue beating until stiff, glossy peaks form.

Fold 1/4 of the meringue into the lemon filling; pour filling into pie shell. Cover pie with remainder of meringue, sealing to edge of shell. Bake on middle shelf of oven at 350 degrees until meringue is browned, about 12 minutes. Cool thoroughly; chill.

Coconut Custard Pie

> 3 eggs, slightly beaten
> 1/2 cup sugar
> 2 cups hot milk
> 1/4 cup coconut
> 1/4 teaspoon vanilla
> 1 pie shell (9-inch), unbaked

In medium bowl, add sugar to eggs. Gradually stir milk into egg mixture. Add coconut and vanilla. Mixture will be thin.

Pour into pie shell. Bake at 400 degrees for 20 to 25 minutes, or until knife inserted in center comes out clean.

Pumpkin Pie

>3 eggs
>$1/2$ cup sugar
>1 can (15 ounces) pumpkin
>1 cup milk
>1 tablespoon molasses
>$1/2$ teaspoon ground cinnamon
>$1/8$ teaspoon ground cloves
>$1/8$ teaspoon ground allspice
>$1/8$ teaspoon ground ginger
>$1/8$ teaspoon salt
>1 pie shell (9-inch), unbaked

In large bowl, add sugar to egg and beat well. Add pumpkin, milk, molasses, spices, and salt. Whip to a smooth custard. Pour into pie shell.

Bake at 425 degrees for 10 minutes; reduce heat to 350 degrees and bake 45 minutes longer, or until knife inserted in center comes out clean. Serve with whipped cream.

Banana Cream Pie

>2 cups milk
>10 tablespoons sugar
>1 tablespoon butter
>$1/4$ cup cornstarch
>3 tablespoons cold milk
>4 egg yolks, beaten
>2 drops banana extract
>5 egg whites, divided
>$1/4$ teaspoon cream of tartar
>6 tablespoons sugar
>2 bananas
>1 pie shell (9-inch), baked

In medium saucepan, combine 2 cups milk, sugar, and butter; bring to a boil.

In small bowl, dissolve cornstarch in 3 tablespoons cold milk; stir in beaten egg yolks.

Remove boiled milk mixture from heat, and while stirring fast, add egg yolks. Return to lowered heat and stir without boiling until mixture thickens. Remove from heat and stir in banana extract. Beat 2 egg whites to a stiff froth and fold into cream filling. Cool.

Prepare meringue by placing 3 egg whites in mixer bowl with cream of tartar. Beat at high speed until frothy. Quickly add 6 tablespoons sugar, 1 tablespoon at a time. Continue beating until stiff, glossy peaks form.

Slice bananas into pie shell, pour cream filling over bananas, and cover with meringue, sealing to edge of pie shell. Brown on middle shelf of 350 degree oven for about 15 minutes. Cool completely before cutting.

NOTE: Tester substituted $1/2$ teaspoon vanilla extract for 2 drops of banana extract.

Desserts

Cabinet Pudding-Vanilla Cream Sauce

This dish appeared on a 1929 menu. Truly a gourmet treat—you will be proud to serve it at your best dinner party.

> loaf cake
> 1/2 cup seedless raisins

Fill 6 well-buttered custard cups with pieces of loaf cake cut in small squares; sprinkle with raisins. Pour Custard (see below) over cakes.

Place custard cups in pan of hot water. Bake at 300 degrees until custard is set, about 50 to 60 minutes. Turn puddings into sauce dishes, serve hot with Vanilla Cream Sauce (see below) poured over the top. Makes 6 servings.

Custard

> 3 eggs
> 1/2 cup sugar
> 2 cups milk
> 1 teaspoon vanilla extract

In medium bowl, beat eggs slightly; add sugar, mixing slowly and well. Gradually beat in milk and vanilla.

Vanilla Cream Sauce

> 1/4 cup sugar
> 1/2 teaspoon all-purpose flour
> 1 egg, beaten
> 1 cup milk, boiling
> 1/2 cup cream
> 1/2 teaspoon vanilla extract

In small saucepan, mix sugar and flour; stir in egg and mix well.

While stirring, add hot milk. Place over medium heat and continue stirring until mixture thickens. Then add cream, keeping on heat for just a minute. Strain; add vanilla; stir.

Date Muffins

A tender and tasty dessert muffin.

> 1/2 cup shortening
> 1/2 cup sugar
> 1/2 teaspoon salt
> 2 eggs
> 1 1/2 teaspoons baking soda
> 1 1/2 cups milk
> 2 1/2 cups all-purpose flour
> 1 1/2 teaspoons baking powder
> 1 cup pitted dates, chopped

In large bowl, cream together shortening, sugar, and salt. Add eggs, one at a time. Stir baking soda into milk. Slowly add to creamed mixture.

Sift together flour and baking powder; add. Fold in dates.

Spoon batter into greased muffin tins (do not use cupcake liners). Bake at 400 degrees for 20 to 25 minutes. Makes 14 muffins.

Shortcake Biscuits

> 2 cups all-purpose flour
> 1 teaspoon salt
> 2 teaspoons baking powder
> 2 tablespoons sugar
> $1/3$ cup shortening
> $2/3$ cup milk (approximately)

Sift together flour, salt, baking powder, and sugar. With pastry cutter, cut in shortening until it is of crumb consistency. Stir in enough milk to make a soft dough. Knead 20 seconds on a lightly floured pastry board.

Roll dough to $1/2$-inch thickness. Cut with a 3-inch biscuit cutter. Bake in ungreased 9-by-13-inch pan at 450 degrees for 12 minutes. Makes 8 biscuits.

Fritters

> $1/2$ cup milk
> $1/2$ cup water
> $1 3/4$ cups all-purpose flour
> $1/4$ cup melted butter
> 2 egg whites, whipped
> $1/2$ cup seedless grapes, halved

Mix milk, water, and flour until smooth. Add butter. Fold in whipped egg whites.

Lightly flour grapes and stir into batter. Drop from tablespoon into fat heated to 375 degrees; fry until done. Makes 18 fritters.

NP Big Baked Apples

Only Washington State apples were used on NP dining cars, both for the fruit's superior flavor and appearance and to contribute to the economy of the territory it served. For Big Baked Apples, the variety specified was Rome Beauty baking apples. When these were not available, Delicious apples were considered a suitable substitute, although they were baked in a slower oven for a longer period of time.

> 4 large Rome Beauty apples
> $1/2$ cup brown sugar
> 2 teaspoons cinnamon
> 2 teaspoons melted butter

Core apples; pare 1-inch strip of skin from tops. Place in cake pan.

Mix brown sugar and cinnamon. Fill center of each apple with $1/4$ of mixture. Pour $1/2$ teaspoon butter on sugar.

Fill bottom of pan with $1/4$ inch of water. Bake at 350 degrees until done, about 45 minutes. Baste frequently with juice from pan. Serve warm with cream. Makes 4 servings.

Potato Doughnuts

1/2 cup hot mashed potatoes
1 tablespoon melted butter
1/4 cup milk
1 egg
3/4 cup sugar
1 1/2 cups all-purpose flour
1 1/2 teaspoons baking powder
1/8 teaspoon salt
1/4 teaspoon ground cinnamon
1/4 teaspoon ground nutmeg

Add butter and milk to hot mashed potatoes.

In separate bowl, beat egg; add sugar. Add potato mixture, then add sifted dry ingredients. Mix well.

Chill dough. Roll out and cut. Fry in deep, hot fat (375 degrees) about 1 1/2 minutes on each side or until golden brown. Drain on paper toweling. Makes 12 doughnuts.

NOTE: Tester increased salt to 1/4 teaspoon and added 1/16 teaspoon ground ginger.

NP Devil's Food Cake #1

1/2 cup butter, softened
1 cup sugar
4 large eggs
1 cup milk
1/2 teaspoon baking soda
1/8 teaspoon salt
1/4 teaspoon vanilla extract
1/2 cup cocoa
1 teaspoon baking powder
1/4 teaspoon ground cinnamon
1 1/2 cups all-purpose flour

In large mixing bowl, cream butter and sugar. Add eggs, one at a time, beating well after each addition.

Stir soda, salt, and vanilla into milk; add to first mixture.

Add sifted dry ingredients, mixing completely. Pour into 9-by-13-inch greased cake pan. Bake at 350 degrees for 35 minutes.

NP Devil's Food Cake #2

1/2 cup butter, softened
1 1/2 cup brown sugar
4 eggs, separated
1 teaspoon vanilla extract
2 cups sifted all-purpose flour
1/4 cup cornstarch
1/8 teaspoon salt
1 teaspoon baking soda
1/2 cup cocoa
1 cup buttermilk
1/4 cup semisweet chocolate, grated

In large mixing bowl, cream butter and brown sugar. Add egg yolks and vanilla; beat well.

Sift together flour, cornstarch, salt, soda, and cocoa. Add to creamed mixture alternately with buttermilk, beating after each addition. Stir in chocolate.

In small bowl, whip egg whites until stiff. Fold into cake mixture.

Pour into 2 round 9-inch greased cake pans. Bake at 350 degrees for 30 minutes. Fill and frost with your favorite icing.

Danish Apple Cake

 6 *large tart apples*
1 ¹/₂ *cups bread crumbs*
1 ¹/₄ *cups sugar, divided*
 ¹/₂ *teaspoon ground cinnamon*
   grated rind of 1 small lemon
   dash of ground nutmeg
   juice of 1 small lemon
 1 *tablespoon butter*
 ¹/₂ *cup water*

Peel, core, and slice apples.

In small bowl, mix bread crumbs, ³/₄ cup of the sugar, cinnamon, and lemon rind.

Butter well a 9-inch glass pie plate. Sprinkle with ¹/₃ of the crumbs, then ¹/₃ of the apples; continue layering in this manner. Sprinkle top with remaining ¹/₂ cup sugar and nutmeg. Dot with pieces of butter; pour water over all.

Place pan of water in oven with cake. Bake at 350 degrees for about 1 hour and 15 minutes. Cool; serve topped with sweetened whipped cream. Makes 6 servings.

NOTE: Tester used 1 teaspoon cinnamon.

Miscellaneous

French Fried Onions

Do try these. You've never eaten a tastier onion ring. Cooks were instructed, "These must be cooked to order and served crisp."

Select onions of medium size. Slice crosswise; separate the slices into rings.

Dip rings in flour, then in milk, and in flour again.

Fry in deep, hot fat until crisp and brown. Drain on paper; season with salt.

Canapé of Shrimp

Cook, peel, and devein desired number of shrimp. Pound fine. Work equal parts of shrimp and soft butter to a smooth paste. Season with just a little lemon juice.

Spread on thin slices of freshly made toast. Trim; cut into 1-inch-wide strips.

Garnish edges with chopped whites and yolks of hard-boiled eggs. Garnish centers with thin slices of stuffed olives.

Banana Scallops

Peel and cut a banana in 1-inch lengths. Flour; dip in thin egg wash; bread in corn flake crumbs.

Fry for 2 minutes in deep, hot fat. Drain on paper towel.

Maître d'Hôtel Butter

In small bowl, stir ¼-pound of soft butter. Using silver fork, work in juice of 1 lemon and a little chopped parsley. Season with salt and cayenne pepper to taste. Keep refrigerated. Serve piece of butter on fish.

Cottage Cheese Relish

2 cups cottage cheese
  cream
¼ cup finely chopped green pepper
1 tablespoon finely chopped pimientos
1 tablespoon grated onion
¼ teaspoon celery seed
  cayenne pepper
  paprika
  salt
  sugar

Reduce the cottage cheese with a little cream. Stir in green pepper, pimientos, onion, and celery seed with a kitchen fork. Season with cayenne pepper, paprika, salt, and sugar to taste. Serve on a lettuce leaf.

Braided Spaetzles

Allow extra preparation time for drying and braiding.

1 egg
½ teaspoon salt
2 tablespoons cream
1 cup all-purpose flour, sifted

In small bowl, beat egg well. Add salt, cream, and enough flour to make stiff dough.

On floured surface, roll dough until thin. Let stand for 20 minutes.

Lightly flour surface of dough; roll up. Slice ⅛-inch wide. Unroll strips; braid 3 strips together. Cut braided strips into 1 ½ inch lengths, pinching ends together.

Dry spaetzles on bread board for 3 hours. Drop into boiling soup or salted water, cook for 15 minutes. Makes 3 cups uncooked spaetzles.

Caramel Sauce

Appropriate for almost any kind of pudding or ice cream.

1 cup corn syrup
1 cup brown sugar
3 tablespoons butter
1 cup evaporated milk

In 3-quart saucepan, combine first 3 ingredients. Bring to boiling point, boil 5 long minutes. Remove from heat, add evaporated milk. Return to heat and again bring to a boil. Remove from heat. Let cool slightly and use, or place in jar and keep in refrigerator.

When ready to use, place over hot water until it is thin again. Keeps several weeks in refrigerator. Makes 2 ½ cups.

Hot Rum Sauce

½ cup butter
1 cup brown sugar
1 tablespoon all-purpose flour
½ cup boiling water
⅓ to ½ cup rum (or 1 tablespoon rum extract)

In small saucepan, place butter, brown sugar, and flour. Blend thoroughly. Add boiling water; cook over low heat until mixture is clear. Remove from heat. Add rum. Serve immediately on pound cake or other desserts. Makes 8 servings.

Pickled Mushrooms

We have been asked to include the recipe for pickled mushrooms, which was one of the items served on the popular hors d'oeuvres tray. The fact is, the NP purchased them already pickled. These mushrooms are still available from Lehmann Farms in Spring Park, Minnesota.

Index

Recipe Index